Traditions
of Lancashire
Past and Present

Compiled and Edited
by
James A. Roby

OWL
BOOKS

First published October 1991 by
Owl Books,
P.O. Box 60,
Wigan WN1 2QB

ISBN 1 873888 00 7

Designed and typeset by
Graphic Design Ltd., Wigan.

Printed and bound in Great Britain.

Body text typeset in 11$\frac{1}{2}$ on 13pt Century Schoolbook.

INTRODUCTION

For many years I have tried to find, without success, a book like this. An informative as well as an entertaining book about Lancashire's past as well as its present. Not a dry-as-dust history book, but one which also tells of individuals, good and not-so-good, who have contributed richly to our Lancastrian heritage.

The County Palatine of Lancashire has a legacy of traditions and customs, whilst illustrious worthies (as well as villains), litter the pages of history. Nowhere in England is there such a rich store of characters and humorous tales as to be found in Lancashire.

The evil in man has, sadly, also found an outlet in Lancashire and to dwell on some of the tortures and punishments once carried out in the name of the law in Lancaster Castle, to this day, can cause ordinary mortals sleepless nights. Additionally, deprivation caused by the corruption of power and wealth has, in the past, created untold social evils and personal misery.

Suffering via the subjugating feudalism of the Normans throughout the 11th and 12th centuries, the cruelties perpetrated throughout the civil wars in the 17th century, and the degredation for many, caused by the Industrial Revolution of the 18th century, have each contributed to moulding the character of a people known throughout the land for their generosity, friendliness and sense of humour in adversity.

* * * *

All the contributors love Lancashire. Some are themselves published authors, whilst some simply enjoy reading and writing about the region historically known as Lancashire.

Keith Johnson of Preston, an avid amateur local historian and author, has contributed an article to celebrate the 1992 historical Preston Guild.

Albert Winstanley of Bolton, veteran touring cyclist and author, is deeply interested in all matters of local history, legends and folklore. He tells us fascinating true tales about Lancashire houses with 'skulls' together with the completely contrasting story commemorating the death of Francis Duckworth, composer of the much-loved hymn tune 'Rimington', who died just 50 years ago.

Cedric Robinson H.M. Guide to the Kent Sands of Morecambe Bay, has submitted the dramatic account of the dangerous "Oversands" route which for centuries connected Lancaster with the North Lancashire town of Ulverston.

Sally Wallbank of Burscough, near Ormskirk, a gifted expert on the paranormal, has contributed our ghostly tales about Lancashire and in particular about Chingle Hall at Goosnargh, near Preston, reputed to be the most haunted house in the whole of England.

Herbert Worsley of Lowton, near Warrington, farmer and author of two books, has contributed an excellent autobiographical account of his farming family and many of the changes in working practises throughout his family's seven genenerations.

Frank Bamber of Sutton, St. Helens, is a well-known local social historian and member of Sutton Historic Society. His story of 30-stone "Owd Bally" Whittaker deserves to be permanently recorded.

Excellent contributions have also been submitted by:

Ellen Callon, of Haydock, St. Helens; Bob Dobson, of Blackpool; Keith Hollinshead of Wigan and Bill Thomas, of Newton-le-Willows.

Finally, I do hope you will enjoy reading 'Traditions of Lancashire Past and Present just as much as I have enjoyed compiling it.

                                        J.A. Roby, August, 1991.

ACKNOWLEDGEMENTS

My thanks are due to the following writers: Ellen
Callon of Haydock; Bob Dobson of Blackpool; Lilian
Harwood and Amelia Fairhurst of Tyldesley; Lilian Hart
of Bolton; Keith Hollinshead of Wigan; Keith Johnson of
Preston; Cedric Robinson, H.M. Guide to the Kent Sands
of Morecambe Bay, Grange-over-Sands; Bill Thomas of
Newton-le-Willows; Christine Thistlethwaite of
Rimington, Clitheroe; Sally Wallbank of Burscough;
Albert Winstanley of Bolton and Herbert Worsley of
Lowton, Warrington.

Thanks are also due to the following for providing
additional information or materials for the following
stories:

Skulls in Lancashire Houses: The Reverend
Secretary, Wardley Hall. *"Owd Bally" Whittaker:* St.
Helens Local History and Archives Library. *Once Every
Preston Guild:* The Harris Reference Library, Preston.
The 'Patter' of Scandal and Murder Most Foul: District
Central Library, Pendle. *There's More to Lanky Than
Meets the 'Een':* Peter Jackson of "Nostalgia", Blackpool
for permission to reproduce the photograph of Samuel
Laycock. *The Perilous Journey from Lancaster
"Oversands":* District Central Library, Lancaster;
Lancaster City Museums; Lancaster University Library
and Ron Sands of Lancaster Tourism. *For Whom the Bell
Tolls in the Fylde:* The Director of Community Services,
Wyre Borough Council; The Evening Gazette, Blackpool.
The Melody Born of Pendle: The Lancashire Library,
Pendle.

The frontispiece line illustration and also on page 46
are from Edwin Waugh's *Poems and Songs*, first
published in 1859.

PUBLISHER'S NOTE
Boundary changes and partition to the area known historically as Lancashire became effective in April 1974. As the
title of this book suggests, *Traditions of Lancashire—Past
and Present*, will contain many articles of historical interest. It has therefore been our policy when seeking material
for publication to consider only Lancashire's historical
county boundaries.

CONTENTS

CONTENTS

Lancashire
Houses with
Skulls

by Albert Winstanley

FROM my cottage garden I can look down to where there once stood a centuries old white-washed farm. I mourned its passing together with the equally old smithy and coach-house that stood nearby, for apart from being echoes of the leisurely age in which they were built, the farm was the setting of a grim and macabre story linked with two Lancashire skulls.

Most of Lancashire's ancient halls and great houses are saturated with traditions and legends, and many can offer visible evidence to lend colour. But—houses with skulls are something quite different. The fact that such grim exhibits are still preserved makes the stories surrounding them all the more vivid and lurid.

The farm that formerly faced my garden was but a small one—its name Timberbottom Farm, and flowing behind is the Bradshaw Brook, taking its name from the village near Bolton.

Long years ago, the two skulls were found in the Bradshaw Brook by a past occupant of the farm, who out of idle curiosity took them inside. Alas, that was his undoing, for from that moment strange things began to happen. Heavy footsteps were heard echoing down the stone-flagged passage of the farm at night. Doorknobs and latches rattled—but when the unfortunate farmer and his wife began to be vigorously shaken by unseen hands when in their beds, the hauntings became intolerable.

A solution had to be found, and the skulls were buried in the consecrated ground of Bradshaw Church, but to no avail. The skulls were then removed to Bradshaw Hall, the once imposing home of the Hardcastles, a noted family of the district. There the skulls were placed on the family bible and happily all ghostly visitations ceased.

When Bradshaw Hall was demolished many years ago, the skulls still resting on the Hardcastle bible were taken to Turton Tower, where they have remained ever since. Woe betide anyone who moves the skulls, for the "visitations" recur at Timberbottom—and I would not relish disturbed nights.

Some say the skulls are those of two thieves who were disturbed when robbing the farm and were killed. Another story is that they are the skulls of man and wife—the man murdering his wife and then committing suicide later. The last occupants of the farm were good neighbours (Mr. and Mrs. Heywood) and I still vividly remember their scared faces as they related their experiences, especially on one occasion when the mounting on one skull was damaged during 'dusting' at Turton Tower and had been sent to Preston for repair. I was on the spot too, when Mr. Heywood in desperation was digging up part of the flagged passage in his farm, to see if anything was buried underneath!

* * * *

I became fascinated with the stories of Lancashire houses that still retained skulls; one of them was Wardley Hall, near Manchester, which for more than two centuries has been known as the "House of the Skull".

I found the hall tucked away down a leafy lane, entirely out of keeping with its present day surroundings. The present building was built by Thurston Tyldesley during the reign of Edward VI (1547-1553). In its hey-day it was moated and entrance was by drawbridge.

I was given a ready invitation to enter and found the

Wardley Hall, near Manchester, tucked away down a leafy lane.

emphasis was on the quality and sturdiness of old English oak. On ascending the stairs I paused after a few steps and there resting within a glass-fronted niche was a centuries-old human skull. Here, I was told, it had rested for over 250 years and was the skull of Edward Ambrose Barlow, O.S.B., a Benedictine monk, who was martyred at Lancaster in 1641.

Edward Barlow (he took the name Ambrose on becoming a Benedictine monk) was born in Manchester in 1585. Wishing to study for the Roman Catholic priesthood, but unable to do so in this country because of religious persecution, he went first to Seminary at Douay in France and then the English College at Valladolid in Spain, where he was ordained priest, before returning to England in 1615, to minister to those who still kept faith in the area between Manchester and Liverpool.

Noted for his saintliness and humility, he carried out his duties on foot, his two main Mass Centres being Wardley Hall, and Morleys Hall in the parish of Leigh. While

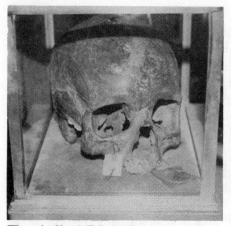

The skull of Edward Ambrose Barlow, Benedictine monk, who was martyred at Lancaster in 1641.

he was recovering from a severe illness, he celebrated Holy Mass on Easter Sunday, 1641, in Morleys Hall for about 200 of the faithful, when a local clergyman "an ardent protestant", some say the Vicar of Eccles while others say the Vicar of Leigh, heard of Ambrose's presence and led a mob of 400 people to apprehend the "Popish Priest". Ambrose was warned of their approach but refused to abandon his people. He was arrested and taken to Lancaster Castle escorted by 60 men.

After four months in Lancaster Gaol, he was brought to trial and accused of being a Catholic priest "and at no time denied the charge". After two days he was found guilty and condemned to be hanged, drawn and quartered. The following day, on 10th September, 1641, the sentence was carried out; he was placed on a hurdle and drawn to the place of execution carrying a small wooden cross, which he had made while languishing in prison.

After Ambrose had been martyred his head was severed from his body, and sent to Manchester on the orders of the Magistrate, to be displayed as a warning to others who still would not conform to the new protestant heresy. However, a relation of Ambrose, Francis Downes "a staunch Catholic" rescued the skull, by night, and guarded it in a secret place in Wardley Hall, where it rested undisturbed for many years.

In 1745, Wardley Hall and its adjacent lands were held

on a life lease, from Lady Penelope of Cholmondley, by Matthew Moreton, who after Charles Stuart's (the Young Pretender) defeat, fell on hard times and decided to pull down a ruinous part of the building to install hand looms for weaving. While this work of demolition was being carried out a wall from the original Chapel was taken down and a casket discovered, containing a skull "furnished with a goodly set of teeth and having on it a good deal of auburn hair".

Ambrose is reputed to have had auburn hair. This does not of itself prove that the skull is that of Saint Ambrose Barlow—who was Canonised by Pope Paul VI on 25th October, 1970—nor does it prove that it is not. However; the following points should be observed and respected:

1. Tradition and local legend hold it to be so.

2. Discovered hidden in the original chapel—suggests that the skull belonged to someone religious, or at least, reverenced by those living here at that time.

3. Forensic tests at the St. Bartholomew's Medical College, in 1960, indicate that it is the skull of a man of Ambrose's age and stature, at that time; that the head has been violently severed from the body after death, and stuck on something like a spike or lance to be carried or displayed.

4. For as long as living memory records, it has been kept, in a niche on the main staircase, and venerated as the skull of the Catholic martyr—Father Ambrose Barlow, of the Order of Saint Benedict.

* * * *

There are many who know the quiet winding lanes radiating from Parbold to Southport, that give a lovely respite from the busy highway, but not many know that as they pass through Mawdesley village, there is a farmhouse, hiding a strange secret in its upper rooms.

When I called at Lane Ends Farm, I was totally unprepared for the mysteries that would be revealed to me. I found the farmer in the yard busy with a tractor and we chatted about farming for a spell. When I mentioned my interest in the story of a Skull, he asked me to follow him.

Entering the farmhouse, I immediately 'ducked' for it seemed there were odd projecting beams everywhere. I followed the farmer up a flight of stairs ascending crazily to mysterious rafter rooms. He told me the structure was mostly 17th century, though several parts had been altered and modernised to cope with farming needs.

The door of a rafter room, cunningly concealed, was opened for my inspection; this had been used as a hidey-hole by a priest. Stranger still, however, was another room, for when the farmer opened the door and I stepped inside, I was amazed to find I was in a small chapel. There was an altar complete with crucifix and various pictures and oddments. This hidden chapel in the gable end of the house was used as a meeting place to hold Mass at the time it was forbidden by law to do so.

I had hardly recovered from my surprise when the farmer took from underneath the altar a glass case, which he handed to me. Inside was a brown skull.

How strange it was to be standing in this hidden chapel room, holding in my hand this grim relic. The skull is said to be that of Father Haydock, who was put to death for his beliefs. He was tried and hanged for high treason along with John Palew, who was the last Abbot of Whalley.

I was shown another little room at the side of the chapel. This was the former sacristy, and low down in the wall was a bricked up 'escape passage' used when danger threatened. To complete the weird picture, ancient robes and vestments still hung there.

Thanking the farmer for his hospitality, I knew the memory of the Mawdesley Skull House would long be with me.

* * * *

At Appley Bridge near Wigan can be found Skull House Lane, and I shall always recall a day when I called on the owner, who in true Lancashire hospitality invited me to enter. First I was shown the house itself, a place of tantalising corners and rambling beams, odd hidey-holes and strange wall cupboards in the thick stone walls. Several stained glass windows in the house depicted a skull—a strange emblem and illuminated by the bright afternoon sun that prevailed.

I was offered coffee and as I was drinking and munching at a biscuit, I admired the massive snaking beam over the fireplace in the living room. With a twinkle in her eye, the owner took from a hidden niche of the beam a cardboard box. I removed the lid and there was revealed a skull, yellow with age but very well preserved. I was a little bemused to be holding my coffee cup in one hand, and the skull in the other, the empty eye sockets and the teeth grinning at me— surely the strangest of Hamlet scenes.

For hundreds of years the skull has rested in this house, and should anyone remove it, besides evil befalling them, it is said the skull will always return to its resting place above the fireplace.

The deaths head skull at Appley Bridge

Before I left the house, I was given permission to take a photograph of the skull and so I gently rested it on a nearby wall in a suitable 'pose'.

* * * *

Throughout the pages of Lancashire history are many

stories of the Civil Wars, and the several battles which took place on Lancashire soil. A tempestuous day in the history of it all was when the Earl of Derby was beheaded in front of the market cross in Bolton in 1651. He is buried in the Derby Chapel in Ormskirk Church. . .in two coffins, a large one for his body and a small one for his severed head.

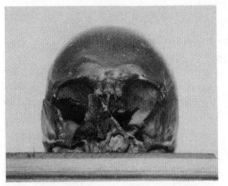

The skull of George Whewell, Executioner of Lord Derby at Bolton in 1651. Whewell was himself executed at a later date and his skull is preserved at The Pack Horse Inn, Affetside, near Bolton.

The executioner was George Whewell who hailed from Affetside village not far from Bolton. When Whewell was chosen to perform the grim task, little did he know that at a later date his own head would also fall, and that his skull would be preserved in the strangest places for such a relic.

Today you can find it in the bar parlour of the homely Pack Horse Inn at Affetside, perched on a small isolated shelf above the well-stocked bar. When I have enjoyed a glass there, I could not repress a smile—for George Whewell's skull also looks over the till—a warning, surely to any would-be thief.

● *NOTE: All the houses, with the exception of the Pack Horse Inn, Affetside, are private residences and are NOT open to the public. Wardley Hall is the official residence of the Roman Catholic Bishops of Salford. Visits by groups and associations may be made by prior arrangement. Enquiries to: The Reverend Secretary, Wardley Hall, Worsley, Manchester M28 5ND.*

"Owd Bally" Whittaker

by Frank Bamber

IT was in 1917, when I first heard the expression "Owd Bally". 'Bally' was the old Lancashire way of describing someone who had more than an ample circumference around the midriff. It was always applied to the male gender, never to the ladies.

I was on my way to Bank House, Bold, near St.Helens, having passed the Boundary Vaults, and crossing the old boundary between Sutton and Bold when I heard a voice calling my name. "Frank!" I turned around and I saw a boy named Sidney Ellison hurrying towards me. He was in my class at school at the old "Sutton Nash". I told him I was on an errand to my uncle's house at Bank House, Bold. He then told me that he lived in Bold and that his parents were the caretakers for William Neil and Sons, the engineering firm, and he lived in the cottage which belonged to the works.

We came to the top of the road where I had to turn left and Sidney had to turn right. Before we left each other we had decided to visit each other during the school holidays. He was to come to my uncle's at Bank House, where the farm was, on one day and I would visit him at Neil's Cottage another day.

The summer holidays had arrived and I was staying at my uncles. Sidney had visited me and we had spent the day at Bank House Farm, and now it was my turn to arrive at Neil's Cottage to spend the day there. We had played around for a time when Sidney said that his mother had made some drinks of cocoa for us both and so that was the first time I entered their house.

At once I noticed that the doors in the house and their openings were much wider than ours at home and at my uncle's. I remarked about this peculiarity to Sidney who smiled and said: "Have you noticed it too? This house was built by Mr. John Whittaker who built the works, and he was so big he had to make the doors and frames so much wider for his own comfort. He was known as "Owd Bally".

We had a laugh about this. It seemed funny to us that a man so fat had to build his house in such a way.

I arrived back at my Uncle Jim's house and told him about Owd Bally and that I had been in his old house at Neil's Foundry. He smiled at me and said he knew John Whittaker well and that he pulled the scales at over thirty stones. He also told me about his horse "Black Bess", which took him from place to place around Sutton, Bold and St. Helens, and he told me it was customary for 'props' to be placed under the carriage step and shafts whenever Owd

Five companions of the White Lion's "long parlour", Church Street, St.Helens, c.1880. Left to right: John Whittaker (30 stones), Joseph Roughsedge, Joseph Jackson (20 stones), William Gardner, Charles Rigby (18 stones). John Whittaker (alias "Owd Bally" Whittaker), was famous for being the heaviest man ever, in St.Helens.

Bally climbed into his conveyance, to keep the float on an 'even keel'.

John Whittaker was born in 1824. My uncle, who was the Farm Bailiff for Bold and Collins Green, was born in 1856, and occasionally came into contact with John, a very able builder and businesman. My uncle told me that John had built the Pear Tree Hotel at Collins Green.

Thirty years later, in 1947, I started to work as a joiner at the British Sidac and became aware of John Whittaker once again. Away from the works buildings, yet still inside British Sidac's premises, where the railway bridge crosses Ellamsbridge Road, stood what appeared to be a large house which was used for storing building materials. Again I noticed the extra width given to the door openings, and then I remembered that it was the old public house called "The Oak Tree Inn", and that John Whittaker was the landlord and licensee there. I remembered it being open as a boy. It must have closed during the 1920s when, or previous to, the silk works arriving in 1926.

John Whittaker built the old Sutton Glassworks and the Oak Tree Inn at about the 1850-1870 period. He was far-sighted enough to realise there would be quite a lot of thirsty men employed at the old glass works and an inn on the premises would be a paying proposition.

In addition to the buildings I have mentioned, John Whittaker was responsible for Daglish's Foundry, St. Helens Junction Station, Boundary Road Baths, Brown Edge Softening Works, Peasley Cross Sanatorium, Sutton Road Pumping Station, The Lingholme Hotel, The Saddle and The Huntsman at Haydock. Also about a score of 150 feet high chimney stacks, showing above the St. Helens skyline was the work of John Whittaker, truly a very remarkable man.

But John Whittaker was also a man full of good humour and was of a jovial disposition, and he had two close companions, Joseph Jackson, a wheelwright and blacksmith near the Fingerpost who had Jackson Street called after him, and who weighed in at 22 stone and 2lb, and Charles Rigby, a wheelwright who weighed 18 stone 2lb. The combined weight of these three heavyweights came within a few pounds of 1000lbs!

John Whittaker's weight remained fairly constant at 30 stones, he weighed himself fairly often at his office and if he found he was putting on a few pounds, he would say: "I'll bout a bit", meaning he would do without for a day or two and would then lunch on one or two sandwiches.

An example of John Whittaker's sense of humour was shown when he heard that Lewis's in Liverpool were offering suits to measure at 30 shillings (150 new pence). He persuaded Mr. Rigby's brother, a man of average build, to go to the shop and ask if they would provide him and his three brothers with suits to measure.

The shopman was delighted to receive the order and invited him to bring his brothers in to be measured, but when Owd Bally walked in with Joseph Jackson and Charles Rigby, he was so taken aback by the amount of cloth that would be required that he sent for the manager. The manager looked at the three of them and realised that if he fitted them out with suits, it would be a great advertisement for the sale of suits from his establishment. "Certainly, we will provide you with suits. We advertise suits at that figure. We will be pleased to serve you all".

The suits were made and the fame of the suits and the story spread to St. Helens.

Owd Bally later donned his outsize suit and made no more ado than to go to his own tailor in St. Helens named Mr. Tickle who carried on business in Raven Street. Owd Bally proudly asked him what he thought about it. Tickle examined the suit closely and asked "Bally" in his typical Lancashire style: "What ast paid for it" and when John said 30 shillings. Tickle turned round to his staff and said with scornful emphasis: "Well all I con say is the bugger's bin bitten", which provoked a great burst of laughter from Owd Bally who repeated it again in the 'long parlour' of the old White Lion public house which was situated in Church Street, St. Helens, saying: "Tickle didn't like the thought of competition from Lewis's at Liverpool".

John Whittaker was a great public character but by no means an eccentric one. He collapsed in a heat wave and died on Monday, 3rd July, 1894, aged 70, and was mourned throughout the town. He is buried at St. Nicholas' Churchyard, Sutton, St. Helens.

In 1987, just 70 years after I was invited into Owd Bally's house by my old school friend, Sydney Ellison, I again visited Bold Park and Kennel Cottage in Hall Lane and also John Whittaker's old home. I measured the doors and found them to be 37 inches wide, which is near enough six inches wider than the average door found in most houses.

Mr. J. WHITTAKER

● *Frank Bamber was born in Sutton, near St. Helens, in 1910, where he has lived all his life. For many years he has made careful notes about the area's past and its many characters, and is a valued member of Sutton Historic Society*

"Once Every Preston Guild"

by Keith Johnson

"ONCE every Preston Guild" is a saying often heard in Lancashire and further afield to describe the occurrence of an infrequent event or incident. Preston Guild is of course a festival that takes place every twenty years and it is due to be celebrated by the inhabitants of the town in 1992.

In the olden days, Preston was famous for its Merchant Guild, granted to it by King Henry II (1154-1189). The memory of this is kept up by "Preston Guild", a festival which has been held every twenty years for many centuries.

On this great occasion the Mayor, Aldermen, and Councillors, and all the societies, trades and clubs in the town joined in processions, which are usually witnessed by thousands of people from other towns. It is also the time when many 'Proud Prestonians', who have settled abroad, return to visit their home town.

The earliest celebration of which we have a clear record occurred in 1328. There were others in 1397, 1415, 1459, 1500 and 1542. At that stage it was decided that the Guild should take place at twenty year intervals and this has been the custom ever since. Neither the Napoleonic War at the start of the 19th century, nor the Boer War at the beginning of the 20th century could halt the historic traditions. In fact the only interruption to the pageantry came in 1942 when Britain, an island fortress, was battling bravely against the forces of Adolph Hitler. Once that particular matter had been settled plans were made to resume the twenty year cycle with a Guild in 1952.

Nevertheless, there was a time when the Guild seemed in considerable danger of coming to an end. Down the years some of the older privileges of the Freemen had vanished for various reasons and with the passing of the Municipal Reform Act in 1835, the last traces of the Guild Merchants' old authority and power had been swept away.

The first Preston Guild due to be celebrated after the passing of the Reform Act was scheduled for 1842. A great deal of argument and debate took place as to whether in the changed circumstances it was worthwhile to hold one then or indeed ever again. After much discussion it was finally decided to continue in the old way, though as a concession to the losing side in the debate, its duration was reduced from the customary fortnight to a week. A special meeting of the Town Council towards the end of June, 1842, confirmed the intention of celebrating the ancient custom in the week following the Feast of the Decollation of St. John the Baptist, and Mayor Samuel Horrocks junior, was appointed Guild Mayor.

If we turn the clock back to that year, the 6th year of Queen Victoria's reign, Preston was no longer an aristocratic little borough but had become a large and populous manufacturing town. Due partly in no small measure to the influence of the Guild Mayor's late uncle John Horrocks, and his own father, Sam, who fuelled a thirsty cotton industry.

The town had thrown off its Parliamentary allegiance

The 1842 Guild, showing Guild Mayoress Eliza Horrocks's Public Breakfast in rooms at the Corn Exchange, at which she entertained "a most select and elegant company".

to the Derby Family. Their mansion, Patten House in Church Street, had fallen into disrepair and been demolished.

The Corporation was no longer a close-knit, self-elected body, but one chosen by a popular constituency in the dispensing of municipal privileges; there was no longer a distinction between freemen and non-freemen. It was this backcloth that the Guild Mayor prepared to carry out the duties entrusted to him.

Prior to the celebrations, the year had been a difficult one for him, with the death of his father, and then in the middle of August 1842, he found himself at the centre of the Lune Street Riot, which will forever be recorded in the town's history. It was with great trepidation therefore that the town moved towards its September celebrations; this being underlined by the fact that the Guild Mayor had to be guarded by the Military wherever he went.

That summer the weather had been particularly fine and on Monday, September 5th, when the Guild Court opened, the day broke with an unclouded sky. The "merrie peal of its far-famed musical bells ushered in the dawn of a new day in the good old town". Many a young heart was beating with excitement and hope, as they looked forward to the pleasures of joining in the amusements, of concerts and balls, and of witnessing or joining in the processions which were to take place. The older folk were thankful of the cheering promise which the sunny day afforded.

Shortly before ten o'clock, the Mayor and Council met at the town hall to open the Guild Books and 'Proclaim the Guild'. There followed a day of festivities with the commencing of a Regatta by the Ribble Yacht Club and a couple of cricket matches on the marsh. That evening there was a brilliant display of fireworks in the market-place, witnessed by a great number of visitors and townspeople. The highlight being a kind of entablature on which were inscribed in many coloured lights the words 'Preston Guild', these were surmounted with a bouquet of Roman candles, which on being discharged, formed a canopy over the whole device, of crimson, blue, green, silver, lilac and orange coloured stars.

On the second day the Procession of the Guild started from the Town Hall led by the Guild Marshalls, featuring the joiners, plasterers, plumbers, glaziers, painters, smiths, coachmakers, printers, glass-cutters, butchers and freemasons. Only the weavers were noticeable by their absence. Other events of the day included a bazaar at St. Ignatius' Church, a wrestling competition for the Guild Belt, while in the evening a grand concert was held at the theatre before a fashionable audience.

The Wednesday belonged to the Ladies and blessed with another sunny morning the town was even more crowded than on the first two days. The Guild Mayoress, Eliza Horrocks greeted the ladies assembled in the Town Hall, and the women formed a procession, to escort her to and from the Parish Church. The procession was headed by the Rifle Band, augmented by a portion of the Trades that had walked the day before and conducted by the Recorder, Thomas Batty Addison, in his official robes. Over a hundred of the towns leading ladies were present, wives and families of people of prominence, including the Birleys, the Pedders, the Addisons, the Swainsons and the Townley Parkers.

Nicholas Grimshaw was the only man to be twice Guild Mayor of Preston (1802 and 1822).

In the evening a full dress ball was attended by over 500 ladies and gentlemen in the saloon of the Corn Exchange. Great crowds gathered to see them arrive in their finery for the Lady Mayoress's Ball.

The fourth day began with the Mayoress's Breakfast in the Corn Exchange rooms and as they ate, the Rifle Band played for their pleasure. The Mayor proposed the health of the Queen, as Duchess of Lancaster, and Mr. Wilson-Patten, M.P. for the County, responded by proposing "The good and standing toast of the Lancashire Witches".

On this day heavy and continuous rain fell, but enthusiasm wasn't dampened as over 2,500 scholars from the Established Church sang several hymns in the Parish Church, and afterwards walked in procession. This day also saw more rowing matches on the Ribble, including the race for the Guild Cup and Horse Racing on the Holme with Mr. King's horse Atalanta winning the Stewards Purse and the Holme Plate. Other events included a concert in the theatre and a ball in the schoolroom of St. Augustine's Church.

Friday, September 9th, the fifth and last day of the Guild, was marked by the entertainment of the school children of the town. It was a pretty sight in the marketplace as the scholars of the Sunday and National Schools gathered with numerous flags and banners.

On this day the weavers, notable absentees on Tuesday, walked through the main streets in procession. After the band came a waggon upon which a weaver, dressed in fancy cap and coat, the product of his own work was engaged in weaving fancy cloth.

Finally, that evening, to bring the Guild to a close, the Costume Ball took place in the Corn Exchange. Described as the most gorgeous of the Guild festivities, the event was held in rooms handsomely decorated with flags and banners. The fancy dresses were of a rich and wonderful variety and included Edward Birley as the Barber of Seville, John Gilbertson as Robin Hood, Edmund Harris in a student's gown and cap, Edward Pedder as a Swiss peasant, Alderman Haydock as a Port Admiral and the Guild Mayor himself in the uniform of a Deputy Lieutenant.

Once the festivities were over much praise was heaped upon the shoulders of the Guild Mayor and his Guild Stewards, John Paley junior, Thomas Monk and George Jackson. It was to be the last Guild that Samuel Horrocks junior would attend; less than four years later he died at the age of 49.

The spacing of the Festival at intervals of two decades, means that each occasion is a significant milestone in the lives of Prestonians. From Guild to Guild the babe in arms becomes the young husband or wife, the mature parent, the caring grandparent; each Guild a landmark in his or her life.

The 1862 Guild was held in the midst of the 'cotton famine', by 1882 the town was becoming industrial. The Guild of 1902 saw the rift with the Derby family healed and the Earl of Derby performing the duties of Guild Mayor.

With the first world war over the 1922 Guild was held in an air of optimism and once again the town seemed under the benevolent rule of 'King Cotton'—one programme remarked that "—if he brought the smoke, he brought the wealth".

Thirty years later, in 1952, the town was fresh from post war celebrations and although many forms of food rationing still existed, the town exuberated colourful pageantry and joyous fun. By 1972 the smokey chimneys of the cotton trade had diminished and smokeless zones abounded. No longer was the town dependent on that industry and its now reliance on engineering skills was reflected in the trade processions.

The 1902 Guild, showing Guild Mayor the Earl of Derby, returning to the Town Hall after a special service in the Parish Church.

31

So on to 1992. Once again Preston's residents, together with a generation who will witness Preston Guild for the first time, look forward with eager anticipation to the pageantry and festivities to come. As we celebrate the 1992 Guild, let us thank those far-sighted men of the 1842 Guild for their determination to continue the great traditions of the Preston Guild Merchants.

● *Keith Johnson lives in Preston. He is an avid amateur historian, in particular about the town's long history, and is the author of 'Chilling True Tales of Old Preston'. (1990). Due to the book's success and two reprints in less than 12 months, it will be followed by 'Chilling True Tales of Old Preston, Book 2' in late 1991. The Preston Guild Year of 1992, will be commemorated with Keith's 'Famous People of Preston'.*

Seven Generations of Farming Worsleys

by Herbert Worsley

JOHN Worsley my great great grandfather, was born in Lowton in the Parish of Winwick near Warrington in the year 1791. How many generations before him had lived in the village I do not know. In the early part of his life he worked as a farm labourer but later, probably because of the very low wages farm workers were paid in the "hungry forties", he became a sand-pit worker, at that time there was a large pit in the vicinity of Sandup Farm, Lowton.

On November 1st, 1819, John married 23-year-old Alice Gregory of Lowton at Winwick Parish Church. Alice was the daughter of a silk weaving family who were reputed to have had a small factory at Lowton Common and were responsible for building the nearby cottages known as Gregory Row.

In 1841 John and Alice were living at Mount Pleasant, Stone Cross Lane, Lowton, with a family of ten children, several of whom were to become farmers, and whose descendants are farming today. By 1851 their son Thomas had emigrated to America to farm there in Wisconsin, and father a now large colony of Worsleys in that country. Son Peter went to Burtonwood where members of his family still farm today, while one of his daughters married Richard Eckersley, who, in the later half of the last century farmed some of the land occupied by the Worsley's of today.

John and Alice died within a few months of each other in February and August of 1865; among village people this seemed to happen quite often, one not being able to live without the other.

Their son John, my great grandfather, married Nancy Hart, a Lowton farmer's daughter at St. Luke's Church, Lowton, on September 11th, 1849. By 1851 they and their baby son, Thomas, were living in the second house at Mount Pleasant. John worked on local farms, contracting to do hedging and ditching or mowing as the seasons came round. In his day he was reputed to be something of a scythe champion, and was highly respected by his contem-

Threshing in the days when labour was cheap and plentiful. There were times when you could barely see through the dust. My job was usually on the 'sacks', taking them off the machine and weighing wheat into two-hundred-weight sacks and oats into one-and-a-half hundred-weight sacks.

Albert Wild mowing a good crop of rye grass for hay, in the 1930's.

poraries—according to an old man of ninety who had known him in those early days. As higher wages started to beckon in the small forges and engineering works that were springing up in Wargrave and Earlestown, there they moved to bring up their family during the next twenty five years. Two of their sons, Thomas, and William my grandfather, became farm workers for the Bridges of Old Hey Farm, Wargrave; the Bridges themselves being natives of Lowton. There is no doubt that this rekindled the love of the land in the two young men who eventually became farmers in their own right. Later Tom, the elder farmed Moss Hall Farm, Burtonwood, until about 1931.

In the early 1880s, John and Nancy took the tenancy of Mill House Farm, (perhaps better known as Nine Arch Farm) Burtonwood, possibly fulfilling a longing for that life they had enjoyed in their early days at Lowton.

In the 1890s their advancing years and difficult times persuaded them to hand on the tenancy to my grandfather William, who in the meantime had married Mr. Bridge's young cousin, Annie Simpson of Lowton, daughter of a farmer and threshing machine proprietor. They were married at Lowton Primitive Methodist Chapel on July 5th, 1882. Incidentally from the days of my great grandfather all the Worsleys and the majority of the arable farmers seem to have been Methodists.

John and Nancy, like John and Alice before them died within a few months of each other in 1905.

William farmed only a few years at Nine Arch Farm, acquiring the tenancy of Highfield Farm, Lowton, in 1902. There the land was of much better quality for the arable farming he wanted to do.

Farming methods were now changing very quickly, William had seen the scythe of his father's day replaced with the mower and the reaper, and had seen the flail replaced by the threshing machine. Now at Lowton he had the selfbinder instead of the reaper, and a corn drill to sow his grain instead of using the 'fiddles' or broadcasting by hand. Times were much better and with an enthusiastic sixteen-year-old son, my father James William, they prospered.

A few cows were kept and pastured on Highfield Moss where they held pasture rights and Annie sold the milk in the village, carrying it to the customers in two sling-cans with the aid of a yoke. She measured it out on the doorsteps as she went along. Unhappily she died in January, 1910, at the age of 55. As a consequence of this James brought his marriage forward so that his new wife could look after himself and his widowed father. James married Clara Ashton, a local girl, at Lowton Primitive Chapel on March 28th, 1910, and continued to farm with his father at Highfield. They were hard working and steady, but unfortunately during the next few years invested their hard earned money in cotton shares. When the recession came in the 1920s all their investments melted away and by 1927, when I was fourteen years old, we had to start again.

Not a great deal of advancement had been made in our

farm machinery at that date, except that we had a potato digger, or spinner, so that in my lifetime we never used the Irishmen who came over each year to harvest the crop. At this time we were just learning how to use fertilizers correctly, all spread by hand of course. Potatoes were still being planted by hand, though at Newton-le-Willows two men, Mr. Hardisty and Mr. Tidgeon, had invented and patented a horse-drawn planter. Mr. Richie the Newton-le-Willow's blacksmith made the prototype. Later Harrison McGregor of Leigh, produced the machine which was marketed all over the country. This machine set the pattern for the many planters that soon followed.

Horse drawn fertilizer distributors were also coming into use; even though we were small farmers these new machines were of great benefit to us. Crop yields continued to rise and progress was being made all through the difficult years before the war.

Grandfather William passed away on 28th of March 1931. The four weeks from the end of February of that year

A harvest scene during the summer of 1940, my father is on the self binder whilst Harry Porler (right) and myself 'stook' a fair crop of wheat.

until my grandfather died, robbed Lowton of three well known local farmers. First John Bent died of Gravel House, who had returned to the village two years before, to spend his last days here. Mr. Samuel Bent and my grandfather attended the funeral; the day was wet and cold and unfortunately Samuel caught cold and died from pneumonia several days later.

I witnessed something that is unlikely ever to happen again: Byroms Farm where Samuel died, is on Newton Road, almost literally, and is no more than three or four yards from the carriageway. During his illness straw was spread thickly on the roadway for a distance each side of the house to deaden the sound of the traffic to prevent any disturbance to the sick man. I understand that in former times when roads were cobbled and the iron-tyred carts rattled by on their noisy way, the practice was sometimes used. In 1931, when the road was asphalted and most of the vehicles were rubber-tyred, it became unnecessary; but I am glad I saw it and was able to record it.

Incidentally John Bent left Lowton House Farm, where I am now living, to farm Wheat Acre Farm, Bold, near St. Helens, in 1902, the same year that my grandfather came back to Lowton. Later John farmed a large acreage at Houghton Towers, Hale.

I mentioned earlier that in the 1930s things progressed favourably for us. Partly, I suppose, because my brother and I were keen young farmers and our father was still in his prime. In 1936 my son was born, the sixth generation of this story. I had married Gladys Mary Warburton whose family on all sides had been farming, some of them for well over a century, and so our son had the blood of all the local farming community in his veins.

A few months before the out-break of the 1939 war, my father was able to buy Highfield. In November of that same year my brother was 'called-up', consequently there followed several years of hard work with the Government

Byroms Farm (top) and Lowton House Farm (from a painting by W.A. Soper) in the early 1900's. Both were built in the late 1600's of hand-made brick, with Yorkshire stone roofs supported by oak beams and spars. Note the relief brickwork pattern at the front elevation of Byroms Farm once a common decorative feature in this part of Lancashire.

exhorting us to grow more and more, and we, like most other farmers had to rely on a casual labour force; sometimes from the local naval camp, other times, prisoners of war.

The opportunity to buy Lowton House Farm came in 1944, it provided a home for my small family and increased our acreage a little. Autumn 1946 saw the welcome return from Wartime service of my brother, who had since married. We realised then that we would have to increase production in order to support three families, and prepared to intensify by aiming to grow more roots and vegetables.

Some months before, father had ordered our first tractor, a new Ford Ferguson (petrol model), but he was never to own it. In January, 1947, mother died, an event which caused my father to lose heart, so much so that by March of the same year he turned the farms over to my brother and myself under the name of Worsley Bros. The new tractor was eventually delivered with all the necessary hydraulic implements, it was like a miniature revolution and enabled us to substantially expand our vegetable growing.

For a while we kept three working horses, but soon there was another tractor and one less horse, so that by 1953 the horses had disappeared altogether; being replaced by three tractors and a tool frame called a Bean tractor.

At this period there were 70 acres in row crops of one sort or another and all the time we were looking to expand. A neighbour observing this, offered us his land. We readily accepted. Ten years later our immediate neighbour sold his farm to us, enabling us to do away with the numerous small fields, making the holding a much more viable unit. My son was brought into the partnership and is the fourth generation to live at Highfield.

The first combine harvester on this farm was bought in 1960 along with grain drying and storage facilities, it was a tremendous change to transfer in one year from the 'sheaf and stook' method, and what a relief it was to have no winter threshing.

For twenty or more years after the War a large variety of crops were grown, including most of the brassicas, potatoes, swedes, sugar beet, peas, and beans, for marketing and canning. All these crops at that time needed a lot of casual labour which was becoming increasingly difficult to find, so that now the cropping had been adjusted to cereals, oilseed rape, and potatoes most of which are washed on the farm. An area of strawberries are grown, a crop introduced by my son Peter in about 1970. Peter married Madge Ruffley in 1958 and moved into Highfield Farm. My father died in the same year—content in the knowledge that his family were carrying on the same tradition.

Peter and Madge's two children are the seventh generation spanning the 200 years since my great great grandfather John Worsley was born. Gillian our granddaughter was born in 1961 and Robert our grandson in 1965. Robert, although trained as a draughtsman is now carrying on in the family business enthusiastically following in the footsteps of his ancestors.

As each generation passes the changes, in agriculture, as with everything else, seem to gather momentum, even though those working on the land are fewer and fewer as the years go by. I wonder what will be the farming scene in South Lancashire when Robert, in turn, hands on to his children?

● *Herbert Worsley has written and published two books 'Family Furrows' (1986) which tells the story of his farming family throughout seven generations and 'The Dwindling Furrows of Lowton' (1988), which tells about farming methods as practised in South Lancashire for over 70 years. Details can be obtained from: H. Worsley, Lowton House Farm, Newton Road, Lowton, Warrington. WA3 1PL.*

The "Royal Sport" of Cock Fighting

by James Pennington

The cockpit claims a name,
Of a sport gentile, and called a royal game,
Now see the gallants crowd about the pit,
And most are stock'd with money more than wit;
Else sure they would not with so great a stir,
Lay ten to one on a cock's faithless spur.

The cockpit in Cockspur Street, Liverpool, was crowded to capacity by people of all classes gathered to see "the great main of cocks fought between Thomas Townley Parker, Esquire, of Cuerden, near Preston, and John Clifton, Esquire, of Lytham, to be fought on Easter Monday, April 5, 1790, and the three following days—to show forty-one cocks each. Ten guineas each battle, and two hundred guineas the main".

At the end of the three days, colossal sums of money had been lost and gained in the betting on fights, often to the death, of the two gentlemen's fearless fighting cocks.

Law abiding folk of the 20th century can have but a faint idea of the sport of cock-fighting of two centuries ago. Not that the sport has entirely disappeared from our midst. In Lancashire, as in other places, there are still groups of participants of this once royal sport, clandestinely gathered to ensure it is not allowed to see 'light of day'.

Information on the 'pastime' was printed in a book published in 1674, titled *The Complete Gamester*, in which the writer claimed: "It is a sport or pastime so full of delight and pleasure, that I know not any game in that respect which is to be preferred before it".

The writer then went on to say that the selection of a fighting cock consisted of just four things: "Shape, colour, courage and a sharp heel".

In the 18th century, hardly a town in England was without its cockpit. In Lancashire, Manchester and Liverpool were the chief centres, each city having four cockpits. Smaller Lancashire towns and villages too often had an official cockpit.

The thirteenth Earl of Derby had a breed of cocks that was famous throughout the county. It is recorded of him that he was so extremely fond of the sport as to have cocks fighting on his counterpane to amuse him when he was ill in bed. The training of his birds was carried out with great care; they had their wings and tails trimmed, and were made to spar daily, pads like small boxing-gloves being tied to their heels, in order that they should not mark each other.

There is an account of a cockfight at Newton-le-Willows on 14th June, 1753, when "Mr. Peter Legh fought Mr. Basil Eccleston a main of cocks, which was won by Mr. Legh in one battle."

In the *Sporting Magazine* of 1825, another fight is recorded:

"The Newton Races were well attended this year. The main of cocks (11 battles for 10 guineas each, and 100 guineas the main) remains undecided, from a dispute that arose during the ninth battle, each side having previously won four. One of the cocks was killed and, while counting him out, the other ran away. Each party claiming, and neither giving way, the main was not proceeded with."

Hogarth's 'Cockpit Royal', engraved in 1758. At that time "the royal sport" was in its ascendancy.

Even though prohibited by Edward III and Henry VIII, Henry himself had a royal cockpit. Cromwell put a stop to cock-fighting for a time but it soon revived after the Restoration. James I and Charles II were particular enthusiasts; it was largely through their example that the sport was closely followed by the gentry. So popular was the sport, that many towns and villages without an official cockpit, often used churchyards for fights, and in some cases the churches themselves.

"Rules for Matching and Fighting of Cocks" had been in practise ever since the reign of King Charles II (1660-1685), and were set-out in the *Manchester Racing Calendar* from 1760 to 1800:

1. To begin the same by fighting the lighter pair of cocks

which fall in the match first, proceeding upwards towards the end that every lighter pair might fight earlier than those that are heavier.

2. In matching, with relation to the battles, it is a rule always in London that, after the cocks of the main are weighed, the match-bills are compared.

3. That every pair of dead or equal weight are separated, and fight against others; provided it appears that the main can be enlarged thereto.

During the reign of George IV (1820-1830), artificial spurs, about one-and-a-half inches long, made of steel or silver came into use. These were either like a curved blade or spike and were bound to the cock's shanks. The cocks, which by nature are combative, usually fought until one was killed. Only very occasionally did a badly battered cock wish to retire, and made its intention clear by raising its hackle. The underpart of a cock's hackle is edged with white feathers and from this came the expression "showing the white feather"—meaning cowardice.

Ultimately society increasingly considered cock-fighting to be a cruel and barbaric sport, as also was the case with bear baiting, so that by 1849, it was abolished by statute of law and included a £5 penalty for every proven offence.

Pit ... Ticket

The 'Patter' of Scandal and Murder Most Foul

AFTER the execution of murderers, whose crimes had attracted much popular attention, and before the introduction of cheap or even 'free' newspapers, 'catchpennies' did a roaring trade. Usually consisting of one single broadsheet about the same size as a modern periodical magazine, the contents were usually written in prose or verse for reading or singing out aloud to the general public.

The sheets generally incorporated an illustration at the top—the same illustration being used for countless different reports—irrespective of the account of the circumstances of the crime. More often than not, the illustration consisted of a rough drawing of the gallows with a figure hanging.

Crowds would often gather round to hear the 'patter' as

it was called and a clever 'patterer' was guaranteed a ready sale of the broadsheets.

The centre of production and publishing of these broadsheets was a place called Seven Dials in London and the monopoly for production of them in the early 19th century was held by a character with the name of Jemmy Catnach—from where the name 'catchpenny' arose.

Although 'catchpennies' were published and printed in London, their biggest sale was in the North of England—and especially in Lancashire.

One of them, "Th'Owdham Chap's Visit to th' Queen",

An early Victorian engraving of an old 'patterer' at work. As well as selling broadsheet ballads, 'patterers' would often sell a variety of smaller items such as 'chapbooks', pins, needles, threads, laces, bodkins, thimbles and hooks and eyes, etc.

One of Lancashire's most celebrated ballad-singer 'patterers' was Robin O' Green of Burnley. One of his well-known ballads was 'The Burnley Hay-makers' which he often sung in the late 1700's. Our illustration of Robin is taken from a contemporary engraving, below which is stated : "Drawn from life. Printed for John Robinson as the act directs, 2nd October, 1780."

relates in dialect, how the subject of the story went to London soon after the birth of the Prince of Wales (King Edward VII), and met Queen Victoria, the Prince Consort and the infant Prince at Buckingham Palace.

On another broadsheet was a ballad entitled: "Miles Weatherhill, the Young Weaver, and his sweetheart Sarah Bell"; the story of a young man who was executed at Manchester for the murder of his sweetheart. The girl was a servant at Todmorden Parsonage, and because he was refused permission to see her, Weatherhill made an attack upon the inmates of the house, killing two of them. The writer of the following doggerel was clearly in sympathy with the murderer, for he says:

"Three innocent lives has been sacrificed,
And one serious injured all through true love.
If they'd not been parted, made broken hearted,
Those in the grave would be living now;
And Miles would not have died on the gallows
For slaying the maiden and Parson Plow.

And all good people, oh, pray consider
Where true love is planted, there let it dwell;
And recollect the Todmorden murder,
Young Miles the weaver, and Sarah Bell".

A broadsheet on the Wigan 'Button Pit' murder in 1863 related the examination and confession of John Healey, and summed up the revolting and cruel murder as follows:

"John Healey is my name,
It was strong whisky did my head inflame,
With four companions at their desire,
At Button Pit, near Wigan,
To thrust poor James Barton in the furnace flames of fire".

A very popular form of the 'catchpenny' was that in which gossiping tales, sometimes distinctly scurrilous, which told of Mr. and Mrs.-----, or Mr. and Miss.----- (leaving a blank space for surnames). They generally began, "Near this street", or "In this neighbourhood", and guileless folk would be induced by the 'patterer' to buy them, in the firm belief that they actually referred to happenings in their own district; the task of filling in the names being a pleasing one for those with malicious thoughts.

In 1839, Jemmy Catnach retired from the business of publishing 'catchpennies', a comparatively rich man.

The "Seven Dials Literature", as it was called, continued to be issued by another firm, though they gradually disappeared as newspapers, which had previously been affordable only by the wealthy, became cheaper when 1861 prohibitive duties on newspapers were removed.

The 'patterer' and the ballad-singer, with their crudely printed 'catchpennies' began to slowly disappear from the streets; since newspapers provided fuller and more vivid details of "last moments on the scaffold" and "dying confessions". In addition the general increase in literacy caused them to be regarded with contempt.

J.A.R

William Haydock Lancashire 'Man o' Brass'

by Keith Hollinshead

IN the rural community of Wrightington Bar near Chorley, in 1896, was born William Haydock into a brass banding family.

At the age of seven, he started to play the cornet with the local Wrighting-ton and Heskin Brass Band, and in 1906 at the age of ten, he attended the famous Crystal Palace, London, National Brass Band Contest, in which their band, under the baton of the famous William Hal-liwell, won 1st Prize in the 5th Section.

William Haydock in the early 1970's

After Army service in the 1914-18 war and a short period in Sir Dan Godfrey's Orchestra from 1918 to 1920, con-ducting brass bands became young William Haydock's

Wrightington and Heskin Brass Band in 1906 with the Champion Journal Challenge Cup Trophy and Cornet. They were won as 1st Prize in the 5th Section.Ten years old William Haydock is seated at the front second from left.

major interest; beginning with Wrightington and Heskin Band in 1920. Then after serving further 'apprenticeships' at Weldbank and Leyland Town Bands, he was appointed bandmaster to Abram Colliery (later Bickershaw Colliery), near Leigh, in 1934.

It was with little-known Bickershaw Colliery band, as Musical Director under the patronage of Major Ernest Hart, colliery owner, that William Haydock's immense skill and abilities were to become legendary in brass banding circles. Under Haydock's baton, Bickershaw Band won the country's leading brass band honours.

At short notice, he conducted the band at Alexandra Palace, in 1938, gaining second place to the nationally-known Fodens Band.

The zenith of his brass banding career came in the years 1940 and 1943, when he conducted Bickershaw Band to first prizes at the British Open Championship, held at Belle Vue, Manchester.

Remarkably, under Haydock's baton at all major brass band contests, Bickershaw Colliery Band were never placed lower than fourth.

The recording company, HMV, had by then noticed the band's successes and in 1938, recordings were made and four disks cut. The BBC too, took an interest in the band and recordings became more and more frequent. In fact relationships with the BBC became so good that by 1942, a signature tune called 'Pennine Way' by Maurice Johnstone, of the BBC, was dedicated to the band.

In a letter from Mr. Johnstone to Major Hart, is included the following extract:

"I am sending you a score and parts of a march for Brass Bands which I have just written, and which I should like to dedicate to the Bickershaw Band and its officers, as a mark of my admiration. . ." In August 1948, Maurice Johnstone rededicated the march to William Haydock.

Sadly, nationalisation of the coal mining industry in

Bickershaw Colliery Band in 1938 with William Haydock as Musical Director (centre). Major Ernest Hart colliery owner is to the left of Haydock.

1947, brought about the demise of this by now great Lancashire brass band. Despite many approaches to Haydock by many of the country's leading bands (Black Dyke Mills, Carlton Main, St. Denis and Leyland Motors, to name but a few), he remained relatively inactive.

Eventually, Haydock was invited to form a band at Wigan Boys Club. It was through this that he saw an opportunity to assist young boys in the pursuit of a worthwhile hobby. Wigan Boys' Club Band was thus formed in the late 1940s.

How would a disciplinarian like William Haydock cope with young boys, who, in the main, did not understand a note of music?

The answer was not long in coming. By an extraordinary combination of patience, enthusiasm and disciplined dedication his pupils were soon playing most proficiently and in due course, were themselves, also broadcasting for the BBC.

"Mr Haydock" with some of his pupils in Wigan Boys' Club Band, taken at a church walking day in 1955.

From starting work down the mine at the age of 13 and without any academic qualifications, William Haydock's achievements were finally acknowledged formally by the Brass Band world in 1971, when he was awarded the Diploma of Honour by the National Brass Band Contesting Council of Great Britain. The award stated truthfully and concisely that it was "In recognition of over 67 years service to brass bands as player, conductor, tutor, organiser and counseller. In appreciation of his devotion, enthusiasm and fidelity in sustaining the highest order in the performance of his numerous voluntary duties on behalf of Brass Bands"

"Mr. Haydock", as he was always known with affection and respect by his pupils, died on 29th July, 1983, in his 88th year. At his funeral service at St. Oswald's Church, Coppull, near Chorley, colleagues and ex-pupils played in tribute to this truly great Lancashire 'Man o' Brass'.

● *Keith Hollinshead is an ex-pupil of William Haydock. He lives and works in Wigan as a teacher of brass, and has an extensive collection of brass bands memorabilia, including many letters which passed between William Haydock and Major Ernest Hart.*

There's More to Lanky Than Meets the 'Een'

by John Pinny

EVERY part of England has its dialect and Lancashire is no exception, except that in Lancashire in particular the dialect as spoken throughout the centuries has been kept alive by writings in it as well as by remaining the ordinary speech of the people.

There are broadly three distinct Lancashire dialects—Lancashire north of the Lune, Lancashire between the Lune and the Ribble and Lancashire between the Ribble and the Mersey.

Many of the words have come down to us almost exactly as they were in Old English and are found in the writings of Chaucer, Spenser and Shakesepeare, and keep alive old words that have died out in so-called 'educated speech'. For example *een* for eyes is almost exactly like the *eyen* found in Chaucer's verse.

There are between 2000 and 3000 words belonging to the Lancashire dialect. Most of them are descended from the Old English or Anglo Saxon. About one in forty have come from Celtic, amongst them *cam*, meaning crooked, which is found in Morecambe Bay.

Northmen or Danes settled in great numbers in south-west Lancashire as witnessed by the numbers of place names ending in *by*. As a consequence more than one word in twenty of the dialect words can be traced to Norse, Swedish or Icelandic. An example being *mun* for must.

Much of the respect now attached to Lancashire dialect writing is due in no small measure to early writers such as John Collier ("Tim Bobbin") (1708-1796); Edwin Waugh (1817-1890); Ben Brierley (1825-1896) and Samuel Laycock (1826-1893).

Unfortunately in the past it would appear that the ladies either did not write dialect, or dare I say it, prejudice against the so-called weaker sex barred them from even thinking of publishing. However I am pleased to be able to say that in recent years the ladies have been making up for the past once male-dominated province of Lancashire dialect writing.

A host of ladies have produced good dialect in recent years. Such as the late Louisa Bearman of Bolton, Joan Pomfret of Great Harwood, Margaret Greenhalgh of Leyland, Edna Wilson Jarrett of Euxton near Chorley, to name but a few.

Lilian Harwood and Amelia Fairhurst are both blind and live together at Tyldesley, near Manchester. Recently they wrote and published a book titled "Two in Accord", which consists of 'poems and stories to make you laugh and cry'. Here are two excellent extracts:

SHIFTIN' T'UNIT
by Lilian Harwood

We were settled wheer we were, my pal, Iris an' me, so, not 'avin enough funds fert' bey a little 'eawse, we geet writin', to aw th'eawsin' associations i' creation, wi' little 'ope an' lots o' papper an' envelopes an' stamps.

One Friday afternoon, eawr phone rang, an' I picks t'receiver up wonderin' oo were at t'other end. It were eawr Joan i' Tyldesley, t'place wur I were born, 74 'ear sin'. Eawr Joan, my youngest sister, 'ad tried 'er best fet' ger us a little 'eawse. Speakin' wi' a glow 'er voice towd us thur were a little bungalow fer us i' Tyldesley, if we wanted it! (if we wanted it) indeed! Well, fert' cut a lung story short, we went reawnd eawr future wom, an' we couldna' ger in it soon enough.

When t'dust 'ad settled, thur were furniture enough fer two flats, 'cos we were settin' up wom together fert' fust time. So some were cadged an' a few were sowd an' then we puzzled which road we wanted t'remainin' pieces fert' stond.

Everythin' else were no bother, but when it come to' t'unit, that were a different thing awt'gether. Wust on it were awe t'books, were braille, an' 'eavy, an' we 'umped loose sheets o' Braille manuscripts. (That's wust o'being' writers).

It were put fust int' far corner near t'far winder, loaded wi' awe its cargo o' Braille but, after livin' wi' it fer a few days, we didna' like it, 'cos it were spoilin' t'seawnd o' Iris's stereo, so it 'ad fert' be moved.

When we fust cum, books an' pappers were awe wrapped up i' neat bags, but neaw everythin' were loose.

Sez Iris, "We'll stack 'up ont' leaf table, under t'winder". So we did—big books, an' little 'uns, an' pappers, pappers, an' more pappers, an' it made a bonny stack. It were lovely! Iris at one eend an' me at t'other, we eased t'unit away fro' t' wa', an' it were rockin'. Imagine this unit, six foot 'igh an' three foot wide, wi' shelves as 'ud slot in an' eawt! Well, o' course, we 'ad sense fert' pull awe t'shelves eawt, an' pur 'um ont' floor, safe under t'far winder, an' neaw, we were awe set! Neaw, this bungalow's low-ceiling't', an' we were gooin' nicely across to' t'other corner when we come in collision wi' t'leet, an' set it swingin', so we theawt we'd best 'ave a breather. We were puffin' an' blowin', like a pur o' runaway 'orses, but we were preawd o' eawr progress, an' so we set off again, wi' a will.

Then, edgin' t'unit in t'new lodgins, my back-eend catched one t' o' t' books on t'table, an' tha talks abeawt an avalanche! We were bein' raint on, an' tha ne'er saw such a state of affurs! We were creawched, 'eawdin' t'unit up, an' killin' eawrsel's wi' laughin', while everythin' o't' table cum slip-slidin' on't top on us. We laughed till t'tears ran deawn eawr faces, but we couldna' wipe 'um away! We'ad fert' 'eawd on to t'unit. Talk abeawt "Ang on the Bell, Nellie!"

Well, press on, regardless! Finally, we made it, an' not a cross word between us, which says summat fer eawr friendship. An' neaw t'unit makes us laugh, God bless it an' us!!

ELEGY
Thoughts inspired by the Gulf War by Amelia Fairhurst

Dear Lord, if tha's up theer, 'elp us, i' these
days o' stress an' strife,
We're livin' through another war, costin' both lim' an'
life;
There's someone's 'usband, faether, sons,
Regardless o'race or creed,
'Cos someone wants what isn't his—
Another case of greed.

Fro' century to century,
Science has played its part,
Wi' each succeedin' century
More deadly fro' the start—
Thy world is filled wi' weapons grim,
Unholy an' defiled—
Guilty an' innocent suffer,
Woman, an' man, an' child.

Be it just two little countries,
But the world in battle 'rayed,
Flauntin' the girts of arsenals,
I' deadly thrust displayed;
An' what will t' future prove at last?
An' the dead, an' brocken bodies,
An' the families that grieve?

Great men o' note 'ave talked an' talked,
To a mon as doesn't care,
An' neaw the East is battle-riv'n
By land, an' sea, an' air,
An' thus the panoply of war
Will fight its future eawt,
Until awt' mass o' folk forget
What it was a' abeawt.

Yet, con it be reet that just one mon
Fert' work 'is evil ways?

Subject another country to
Such fearsome neets an' days?
Pillagin', rapin', killin' folk,
Fert' satisfy 'is lust?
Do we do wrung? Do we do reet,
Lendin' eawr vengeful thrust?

Some say we mun; some say we mawnt;
Which way are we fert' foller?
It's a strung source o' argument,
For learned sage an' scholar;
Gen'rals an' adm'rals an' such
Define their ways fert' beat 'im
An' diplomats 'ave done their best;
But nothin' will defeat 'im.

Which way? which way? we cry, O Lord,
'Elp us fert' understond;
Tak' us, thy little childer, Lord,
An' lead us by the 'ond!
Eawr world 'as geet too much for us!
We don' know wheer to go;
'Cos, Lord, for awe eawr cleverness,
There's lots we dunnot know.

If on'y mon could speak to mon
Fro' badness melt 'is 'eart!
If on'y love an' brotherhood
Could play its proper part!
If on'y lust an' war an' might
An' awe its wrung would cease,
Then we could live more close to thee,
An' 'bide in Holy Peace.

Lilian Hart lives at Firwood Fold, Bolton, birthplace of
Samuel Crompton in 1753. She produced poems for the
1979 Bolton Festival which became extremely popular.
Titles include: "My Town Bolton", "That Mon From Firwood", "The Last Tram". Six poems in all were made into
a series of greetings cards under the heading "Greetings
from Bowton", which sold to Boltonians and friends world-
wide.

The following poem will for many older folk bring back
memories of travelling to Blackpool by steamtrain as a
child, for a week's holiday:

TER BLACKPOOL AN' WHOAM
by Lilian Hart

I di ger aw excited, when I were a little lass,
Mi dad...he worked ont railroad an' he gor us a free pass,
I gripped mi muthers hand ser tight, as a looked at aw them faces,
Ther' must 'ave bin hundreds ont station wi' ther' cases,
Mi stomach, it were churnin' o'er, an' nor a word I spoke,
As I waited fer that engine, an' I watched fer aw that smoke,
Then...Theer it were, I spotted it, cumin deawn that track,
I felt a little freetend, I think neaw as a look back,
That greight big shiny engine, puffin' eawt big clouds er smoke,
Cum roarin' intert station ter pick up aw them folk.
Mon were theer int shiny cap, wi' his face as black as cole,
Sweatin' cobs...aw greasy he looked fro workin' in that feigher 'ole,
Yer had't be very careful as yer were gerrin on,
Ther' were a space as yer could faw deawn, so a stuck tight ter mi mam,
Seats inside like couches, aw velvety an' cumfy,
An' pictures ont walls er places eawt int country,
Wi aw sit deawn inside an' mi dad...he dealt wi' th'bags,
Then one mon cum up station wi' a whistle an'a flag,
Ther' were such a shuntin' neighs, an' a screech from' t th'engine theer,
Wi' a reight strung smell of e'oil an' smoke as it jerked us in our cheer,
Off wi went, aw packed in tight, an' movin' fro side ter side,
'I think a con...I think a con' said th'engine on that ride,
Wi seemed bi sit theer ages, then mi dad said 'Theers Tower'
Ee I were excited...'ad nar seen it afoor,
Wi spent a luvly week yer know, and th' sun were shinin' bright,
A broke mi heart went time were up, an' on that Friday night,
Mi mam said 'Home tomorrow, holidays ar o'er, we'll have our last fling
fer this year, an' goo deawn tert South Shore'.
Satday cum, an' th' tears were shed as wi said our last goodby'es,
Then awf wi went tert station, wi' tears in our eyes,
But when a saw yon engine cum shuntin' deawn that track,
A felt reight proud of it somehow...it 'ad cum ter tak us back,
Fer that sayin's reet, I must admit, wherever you may roam,
No matter eaw yo' 'ave enjoyed yersel...
There's still NO PLACE LIKE HOME.

Christine Thistlethwaite lives at Rimington, near Clitheroe. She has published a couple of small books titled "Times and Seasons Rhymes and Reasons" and "Here a Little and There a Little". A short time ago, as a tribute to Francis Duckworth, composer of the hymn tune *Rimington* and one-time resident of the village, she penned the following delightful poem:

RIMINGTON

by Christine Thistlethwaite

Esta 'eard o' Francis Duckworth?
'E'd a grocers shop in Colne
An' 'e wrote a famous hymn-tune
Surely t'finest ivver known
'E wor born in t'eighteen sixties
in Rimington yer know—
Yon's a gradely little village, not far frae Clitheroe
An' as a lad, wi' carefree heart, he'd laiked in't' woods and'
streams
An' larnt o' natures wondrous ways, an' dreamed his boyish
dreams
They lived next door to t'Chapel, in t'shop in Stopper Lane,
An' singin' hymns on Sundays theer—t'little lad wor allus fain
He had a gift fer music, an'so when he wor twelve
they med 'im organist, ter play fer't' services hisself!
His mother died, an 'times wor hard, so he med 'is way to Colne,
Hard work paid off, an' soon he had a business of 'is own
He played on grander organs—music still was all his joy
But 'e oft-times thowt o' Rimington, an' 'is life theer as a boy
'E remembered how his Uncle John—a man, sincere, devout
was moved one day to lift his arms—proclaiming with fervent
shout
"Jesus shall reign, where e'er the sun!—Now, there's a hymn
of praise
Would that the world with Watts great words their myriad
voices raise"
Francis thowt on, an' so inspired, composed a tune so grand,
Surely some angel-scribe stood by to guide his fleeting hand!
An' so it was, one Whitsuntide, in Colne, there rose the sound
of Christian voices swelling up in harmony profound.
In years to come, fulfilling Uncle's prophecy of yore
this wondrous hymn sped round the world, beloved on every
shore,

Tho' Francis wrote some lovely tunes, this truly stands alone
It seems to carry in its heart a magic all its own
Tis many years since Francis went to join the heavenly throng
and carved upon his gravestone is his sweet immortal song
So, when the last 'Amens' ring out,
let earth be joined in one with all the Heavenly Choirs to sing
this anthem — *"Rimington"*

● **To commemorate 50 years since the death of Francis Duckworth, in August 1941, Albert Winstanley has written *'The Melody Born of Pendle'*. Page 96.**

Perhaps it is appropriate to conclude with one or two traditional dialect extracts:

Samuel Laycock was born at Marsden on the borders of Lancashire and Yorkshire in 1826 but came to live in Stalybridge at an early age, where he worked as a weaver until the days of the 'cotton famine'. He eventually retired to Blackpool, where he died in 1893. Like most early dialect writers, he drew on his personal experiences and his popu-

Samuel Laycock (1826-93).

lar 'Bowton's Yard' was no exception. 'Bowton's Yard' (Bolton's Yard) prior to its demolition in the 1950s stood off Cross Leech Street, Stalybridge. In this poem, Laycock describes the occupants of each of the twelve dwellings there.

BOWTON'S YARD
by Samuel Laycock

At number one, i' Bowton's Yard, mi gronny keeps a skoo,
Hoo hasna' mony scholars yet, hoo's nobbut one or two;
They sen th'owd woman's rayther cross—well, it may be so;
Aw know hoo boxed me rarely once an' poo'd mi ears an' o.

At number two lives widow Burns, hoo weshes clooas for folk;
The'r Billy, that's her son, gets jobs at wheelin' coke;
They sen hoo cooarts wi' Sam-o'-Ned's, 'at lives at number three;
It may be so, aw conno tell, it matters nowt to me.

At number three, reet facin' th'pump, Ned Grimshaw keeps a shop;
He's eccles cakes an' o, does Ned, he 'at boath soft an' hard,
An' everybody buys off him 'as lives i' Bowton's Yard.

At number four Jack Blunderick lives; he goes to th'mill an' wayves;
An' then, at th'weekend, when he's time, he pows a bit an' shaves;
He's badly off, is Jack, poor lad! he's rayther lawm, they sen,
An' his childer keep him deawn a bit, aw think they'n nine or ten.

At number five aw live misel', wi' owd Susannah Grimes,
But dunno like so very weel, hoo turns me eawt sometimes;
An' when aw'm in ther's ne'er no leet, aw have to ceawer i' th'dark;
Aw conno pay mi lodgin' brass becose aw'm eawt o' wark.

At number six, next door to us, an' close to th'side o' th' speawt,
Owd Susie Collins sells smo' drink, but hoo's welly allus beawt;
An' heaw it is, ut that is so, aw'm sure aw conno tell,
Hoo happen mak's it very sweet, an' sups it o hersel'.

At number seven ther's nob'dy lives, they laft it yesterday,
Th'bum-baylis coom an' marked the'r things an' tok 'em o away;
They took 'em in a donkey cart—aw know nowt wheer they went—
Aw reckon they've bin ta'en an' sowd becose they owed some rent.

At number eight—they're Yorkshire folk—ther's only th'mon an' th' wife,
Aw think aw ne'er seed nicer folk nor these i' o mi loife!
You'll never see 'em foin' eawt, loike lots o' married folk,

They allus seem good-temper't like, an' ready wi a joke.

At number nine th'owd cobbler lives, th'owd chap ut mends mi shoon,
He's gettin; very wake an' done, he'll ha' to leeov us soon;
He reads his Bible every day, an' sings just like a lark,
He says he's practisin' for heaven—he's welly done his wark.

At number ten James Bowton lives, he's th' noicest heawse i' th' row;
He's allus plenty o' summat t'ate, an' lots o' brass an' o;
An' when he rides or walks abeawt he's dressed up very fine,
But he isn't hawve as near to heaven as him at number nine.

At number 'leven mi uncle lives, aw co him Uncle Tum,
He goes to concerts up an' deawn, an' plays a kettle-drum;
I' bands o' music, an' sich things, he seems to tak' a pride,
An allus mak's as big a noise as o i' th' place beside.

At number twelve, an' the'end o' th'row, Joe Stiggins deols i' ale;
He's sixpenny, an' fourpenny dark-colour't, an' he's pale;
But aw ne'er touch it, for aw know it's ruin't mony a bard,
Aw'm th'only chap as doesn't drink 'at lives i' Bowton's Yard!

An' neaw aw've done, aw'll say goodbye, an' leeov yo' for awhile;
Aw know aw haven't towd mi tale i' sich a fust-rate style;
But ive yo're pleas't aw'm satisfied, an' ax for no reward
For tellin' who mi neighbours are ut live i' Bowton's Yard.

Probably the best known name amongst dialect writers is Edwin Waugh. He was born in Rochdale in 1817 and began his working life as a journeyman printer. His "Sketches of Lancashire Life and Localities" (reprinted from the *Manchester Examiner)* appeared in 1855. A year later his song "Come whoam to thi childer an' me" made him famous throughout the land. He spent his life writing songs, tales and character sketches in the Lancashire dialect, which like his friend, Ben Brierley, filled eight volumes.

The following poem is from his "Poems and Songs", first published in 1859:

Edwin Waugh (1817-90).

WHEN THE SUN GOES DOWN
by Edwin Waugh

When life's glad day is gone,
And the sun goes down;
When we muse all alone,
As the sun goes down.
Oh, the heart is not so light,
When the day is taking flight,
And we feel the coming night,
As the sun goes down.

Oh, the flowers fall asleep,
When the sun goes down;
And the silence is deep,
When the sun goes down;
But the skies of night grow fine,
And the stars begin to shine,
With a radiance divine,
When the sun goes down.

Oh, the curfew bell's tolled,
When the sun goes down;
And the churchyard tower grey
Calls life's children home from play,
At the closing of the day,
When the sun goes down.

Ere the lark sinks to rest,
When the sun goes down,
In his grass-shaded nest,
When the sun goes down;
While the world begins to dream,
Then his evening carols stream
From the gathering starlight's gleam,
When the sun goes down.

So, remote from the throng,
When the sun goes down,
Life's quiet shades among,
When the sun goes down;
In the twilight deepening grey,
At the waning of the day,
Let me sing my little lay,
As the sun goes down.

The Great Broad Oak of Winwick

by Bill Thomas

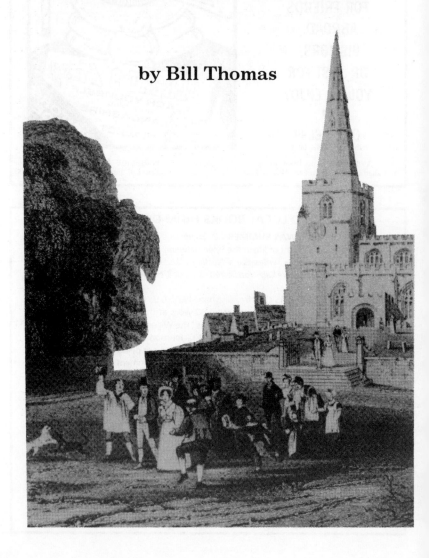

CAPTAIN Phipps Hornby son of the Rector of Winwick, was captain of *The Volage* which had captured a French flag at the Battle of Lissa, in the Adriatic, on 13th March, 1811. It was a battle which was then considered "one of the most brilliant achievements" in the long war with France.

His return home to his parent's cottage at Winwick in August, 1811, after five years absence, was eagerly anticipated by family, friends and neighbours. All were anxious to welcome home the local hero, who had shown such bravery in the service of his country.

To celebrate his return, the village of Winwick was to witness a celebration, the like of which was never seen before or since. A most unusual location for the celebration had already been decided upon. In a field a little distance from the south side of the church stood a magnificent broad oak tree. It covered an area of ground 100 yards in circumference, the lower branches of which extended 99 feet from north to south and 87 feet from east to west. The girth of its trunk at the base was 14 feet, and $11^{1}/2$ feet at a height of 5 feet.

It was beneath this oak tree's spreading canopy of branches on 26th August, 1811, the gentry and yeomen from miles around—one hundred and twenty four people in all—enjoyed a princely banquet. The interior of the great tree was covered with fine white cloth, giving an appearance of a huge tent and the tables were arranged in a semi-circle around the trunk.

Never before at Winwick had there been such feasting, music and speechmaking, and a song was composed especially for the occasion:

> Ye Britons, venerate this tree
> Which forms our verdant canopy,
> Fam'd in historic page;
> Beneath its shade the Druid rose,
> And wak'd the British youth from woes

To true heroic rage.
Forth from their woods they rush'd like
flame,
What time Rome's hostile legions came
They met them at the wave;
And who shall call the conflict vain?
They perish'd on their native plain,
Nor liv'd a race of slaves.
And still the oak, our island's boast,

On 26th August, 1811, one hundred and twenty four people gathered beneath the branches of the broad oak of Winwick, to enjoy a princely banquet.

From hostile foes protects our coast,
Hence are our terrors hurl'd.
Ye Britons, venerate the oak!
Nelson from this in vengeance spoke
And shook th'astonish'd world.
Nelson's no more! Hoste, Whitby live,
Gordon and Hornby too survive,
Enrob'd in Nelson's vest.
"Remember Him!" on Lissa's coast
Said he, who was himself a Hoste,
And thunder spoke the rest.
While th'oak shall flourish in the glade,
What foe shall dare our shores invade?
O lovely tree, increase!
Still spread thy verdant branches far,
Protect us in the time of war
And shelter us in peace.

Sadly this magnificent oak tree was blown down in a gale on 4th February, 1850. It is quite likely that at that time the tree would have been alive long before the present Winwick church was built in 1358, in the reign of Edward III.

Reminders of the celebration day and the Great Broad Oak of Winwick still exist in the church, where there are four wooden benches made from the tree's timber, together with a picture of the banquet.

● *Bill Thomas was born in Newton-le-Willows in 1914, He is a regular contributor of social history to Wargrave church magazine and is a long-serving member of Newton-le-Willows Historical Society*

The Perilous Journey from Lancaster 'Oversands'

by Cedric Robinson

BEFORE the days of the railways, the quickest route from Lancaster northwards to the area known as Furness was across the sands of Morecambe Bay. Though potentially fraught with danger, a quick glance at the map explains why the route known as "Oversands" was popular in the days of the stagecoach.

From Lancaster via Kendal to Ulverston was a distance of 40 miles. Even the new turnpike of 1820, which had to pass the obstacle of a large peaty bog at the foot of Whitbarrow Scar, was still a distance of 34 miles. Over the sands, a distance of a mere 20 miles, was a considerable saving in time and energy for both man and beast.

Coach services scheduled to accommodate the changing tides, ran between hotels in Lancaster and Ulverston. In

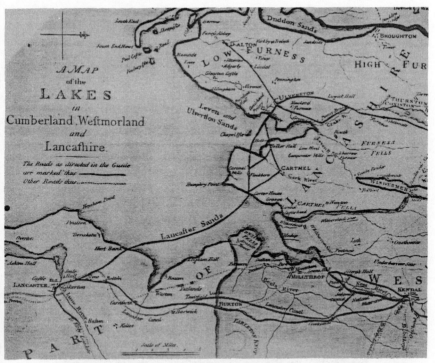

A 1793 map of North Lancashire which clearly shows the "Over-sands" low tide route across Morecambe Bay.

the *Lonsdale Magazine* of 1820 one writer tells of a rude awakening at his Lancaster hotel when at 5 a.m. the coach driver burst into his bedroom shouting: "For God's sake make haste! The tide is down—if you delay we shall all be drowned!"

Documentary evidence tells us that guides for the journey across the sands have been employed since the time of the building of both Cartmel and Conishead Priories in the 13th century. Chapel Island in mid-channel was a resting place, where prayers for safe crossings were offered by the monks who provided the guides.

The post of official Guide to the Sands is many centuries old and was created by the Crown in 1337 after many

Sun Inn, Ulverston.

Cheap and Expeditious Travelling.

The Public are respectfully informed, that an entire New Elegant

LIGHT
POST COACH

Starts from the above Inn, every Sunday, Tuesday, and Thursday, to the

King's Arms Inn, Lancaster.

And Returns every Monday, Wednesday, and Friday,

AT REDUCED FARES

Infides 3s. Outfides 2s.

AND to all Parts of Great Britain, reduced in equal Proportion. It is the only COACH, whereby Passengers can be secured of Places North of *Carlisle*, or South of *Liverpool*.

At the Kings Arms, Lancaster,

IT Communicates with the COMMERCIAL LONG COACH to *Liverpool*, every Morning at 7 o' Clock, to the Crown Inn, Red Cross Street.

ALSO,

A New LONG COACH through *Birmingham* and *Oxford*, to the Saracen's Head, Snow Hill, *London*.

ALSO,

AN Elegant LONG COACH, to *Manchester*, every Morning at 7 o'Clock, through *Chorley* and *Bolton*.

ALSO,

THE COMMERCIAL LONG COACH, every Evening at 4 o'Clock, through *Kendal*, *Penrith*, and *Carlisle*, where it Communicates with all the Public CARRIAGES into *Scotland*.

Performed by J. PRITT and Co.

JOHN CROSTHWAITE, Sadler, Agent for *Ulverston*.

IT ALSO MEETS

The Royal Mail Coach

To *London*, every Afternoon at 2 o'Clock.

ALSO,

THE ROYAL MAIL COACH, to *Carlisle*, every Morning at half past 11 o'Clock.

N. B. The Company Respectfully inform their Friends and the Public, that they will not be accountable for any Parcel, Box, or Package, of any kind, or Passengers' Luggage, &c, more than 5£. Value, if either Lost or Damaged; unless Specified at the time of Delivery, and Paid for Accordingly.

J. Soulby, Printer, Ulverston.

A 1798 Advertisement for Post Coach Travelling "Oversands".

people had lost their lives whilst making the crossing.

In the past the Guides were referred to as The Carters of Carr Lane; the Guides cottage being known as Carter House. It is believed that at one time it was a rule that the appointed Guide had to take the surname of Carter.

After the Dissolution, the Duchy of Lancaster records state:

> "Office of le Carter's office of Leven Sands near Conyshead Lancashire, January 29 1548. The King, etc., all to whom greeting know ye that we by the advice and assent of our Council of our Duchy of Lancaster have given and granted and by these present do give and grant John Harlteley of Conyshead, yeoman, the office of keeper, conductor and governor of our sands near Conyshead aforesaid. . ."

Also, in 1548, a keeper of Kent Sands was appointed by the name of Thomas Hogeson, who had previously been the guide for Cartmel Priory. For this, he received £5 per annum, the 'Carter House' and three closes of land. The Carter House and the three closes of land are still occupied only by the Guide to the Sands.

The terrible perils of the journey "oversands" include quicksands, the ever-shifting terrain of the bay, and most terrifying of all, mist and sea fog, which completely obliterates all landmarks, making the way ahead as featureless as a desert.

To wander lost on the sands is to invite death by drowning.

At the beginning of the 19th century, many years after their disappearance, a horse and man in an almost perfect state of preservation were suddenly exposed to the air. They had perished like many before and many after them would also perish in the shifting quicksands.

Until 1820, stagecoach drivers chose their own route crossing, after that date a guide was appointed to assist them; even so the tragedies continued. The Cartmel registers alone record 141 persons buried there between 1559 and 1800. To record but a few since 1821:

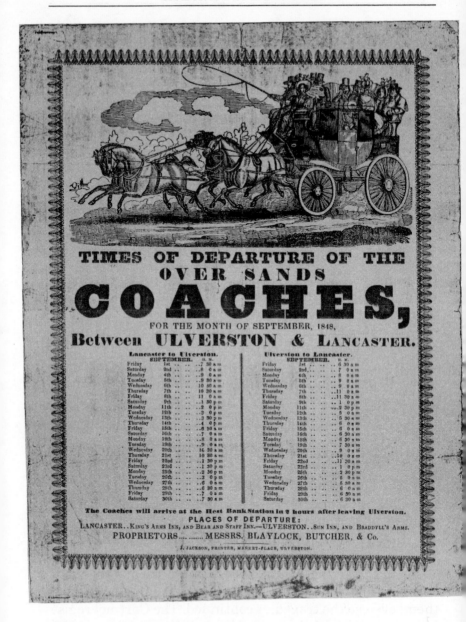

A poster of 1848 advertising the "Oversands" crossing between Ulverston and Lancaster.

"1821—Postchaise lost, close to Hest Bank. Occupant, postboy, and one horse drowned.

1825—Lancaster-Ulverston coach blown over in mid channel; passengers saved, one horse drowned.

1828—Lancaster-Ulverston coach suddenly sank in the sands, passengers saved.

1846—Nine young people returning to Cartmel from Ulverston Whitsuntide fair all drowned. Their cart went into a large waterfilled hole and other travellers on the sands did not even hear a cry.

1857—Seven farmhands going to Lancaster hiring fair found drowned the next day."

The list seems endless.

Nevertheless people were not put off travelling Oversands, it seemed a relatively small risk. Many crossed the sands regularly in the course of business. John Higgins, carrier, regularly went from Lancaster to Swarthmoor Hall, near Ulverston, with "letters, iron ore, hopps, redherrings, books, sugar, vinegar, meat, paper, oysters, phisicall things, and chocoletta".

From Swarthmoor Hall near Ulverston in 1660 travelled George Fox, founder of the Quakers. Then a prisoner, he was accompanied to Lancaster Castle Oversands with "16 troops of horse".

A private letter from a schoolboy, writing home to his mother, after arriving safely back at school after the holidays, states:

"29 January 1786: Dear Mother, I arrived here (Lancaster) safe yesterday evening about 7 o'clock after a rather disagreeable passage; it was very thick all the way, and crossing at the low ford, there was no Carter, so the driver was obliged to take a horse and try the ford, which was very deep for the water was near a foot in the coach, and after that the sand was so exceeding heavy, that we were obliged to get out, and walk three or four miles..."

The earliest coaches to travel oversands were known as 'dillies'. They carried 13 passengers inside and the luggage on top, but were very heavy and frequently became stuck in the sands. Eventually they were superseded by smaller and faster coaches. An advertisement from the *Cumberland Pacquet*, dated 11th September, 1781, states:

> "A Diligence or Chaise, which will carry three persons conveniently, will set out from Mr. Stanley Turner's, the Sun Inn, Lancaster, every Monday, Wednesday and Friday, as the tide will permit, to Ulverston, over the Sands, which is the nearest and direct route to Whitehaven. And the same Diligence will return to Lancaster from Henry Addison's, the King's Arms, in Ulverston, every Tuesday, Thursday, and Saturday. Each passenger to pay five shillings on taking a place for Ulverston or Lancaster. The proprietors assure the public that they have procured a sober and careful driver, who is well acquainted with the sands, and humbly hope that their plan will meet with due encouragement, as this is the most cheap, safe, and expeditious method of crossing the sands to and from Ulverston".

Stagecoaches ran successfully until the opening of the Ulverston-Lancaster Railway in 1857.

The graveyards around the Morecambe Bay area testify to the hazards of the Oversands crossing at low tide, but there were occasions when the journey was so exhilarating that it lived on in the memories of travellers for many years. Eminent writers such as William Wordsworth (1770-1850) and Thomas Gray (1716-1771) described sublime experiences of the kind portrayed in Turner's magnificent watercolour "Crossing Lancaster Sands".

Today, the Oversands crossing is still possible, but only under the safe and experienced conduct of Her Majesty's Guide to the Kent Sands of Morecambe Bay. And the railway that changed the travelling habits of the nation now only takes a mere 17 minutes to link the historic City of Lancaster to the Lake District's main line station at Oxenholme

● *Cedric Robinson is currently H.M. official Guide to the Kent Sands of Morecambe Bay.*

"Crossing Lancaster Sands"
J.M.W. Turner
(1775-1851)

Courtesy Birmingham Museum and Art Gallery.

To celebrate Lancaster's close association with the Lake District, Turner's painting has been reproduced as a folding fine art card by Lancaster Tourism. The card, which is also suitable for framing is available by sending just three First Class stamps to: Traditions of Lancashire, Lancaster Tourism, Lancaster City Council, White Cross, Lancaster, LA1 4XQ.

Tacklers'
Tales

A MONG the many job descriptions of Lancashire cotton mill workers, the 'tackler' became traditionally the harmless butt of many jokes. Tacklers had the job of looking after the loom section problems of the weaving shed. They were mostly honest, industrious men and entirely capable of giving and receiving jokes and just as important, laughing at themselves. As a result many jokes evolved around the Tackler in much the same way as a particular type of joke is, today, aimed at the Irish (Pat and Mick) today. A common joking Lancashire criticism at one time was: "'Ee, th're a reight tackler".

Long before the days of the "wireless" people gathered in one another's homes on a regular basis to tell tacklers' tales. No church concert was at one time complete without the local amateur comedian telling a story about tacklers.

Not surprisingly, in the days long before strict discriminatory laws, joke books called "Tacklers' Tales" began to appear, which proved very popular with the public. The following is typical of the jokes found within their pages:

A Chorley tackler was taking his wife to Blackpool for the first time. They were going to stay with his wife's aunt who lived up north. Getting off at South Shore Station they boarded a tram car. Not knowing where to book to, he listened to what a young lady near to him said to the conductor: "One to Uncle Tom's please", she said. The tackler then said to the conductor: "Two to t'wife's Aunt Mary's please".

***

A Leigh tackler, having courted and won one of his four loom weavers, decided to go and purchase the ring. "Aw want a gradely ring for t'lass awm gooin' t' wed". "Eighteen carat?" enquired the jeweller. To which the tackler answered: "Eytin carrots—no I'm not, I'm chewin' bacca".

***

A tackler entered a public house in Barnoldswick and said: "Con I 'ave a pint on't strap". The landlord said: "Now look here, I am the new landlord and I am determined not to allow any strap, but I'll tell you what I'll do: I'll lend you two shillings until week-end". He then pushed a two shilling piece across the bar towards the tackler. The tackler picked it up, put it in his pocket and began to walk towards the door. At this the landlord shouted after him: "I say, aren't you going to have a drink?" To which the tackler answered: "Nay lad, If tha'll not strap me, then I'll go and spend mi money somewhere else".

***

A Wigan tackler was once asked to find out how many gas mantles in a weaving shed needed replacing. He came back with the answer: "All of 'em; I tried t'lot and they're all soft"

***

A youth, who started a new job as a tackler at a Blackburn mill, was repeatedly late for work from his very first day. After a week the manager called him into the office and asked him if he knew what time the mill started. "No", he answered, "There allus agate when I ger 'ere".

The same evening the tackler was spotted putting on his coat several minutes before the finishing hooter. This time he was more severely reprimanded. "To tell you the truth", he answered, "I didn't like being late at both eends o'th'day".

***

Tacklers weren't always as daft as they were made out to be as the following tale tells:

Two ordinary chaps and a tackler went to collect a second-hand hen cabin. On the way back two of the three were carrying the cabin at opposite ends with great difficulty. Suddenly the two realised the tackler was missing. "Wheer's tackler?" asked one. "I'll bet he's sloped off, 'cos there's work to be done", said the other. "I've not", cried an indignant voice from inside the cabin. "I'm in 'ere, carryin' t'perches".

***

Finally an inspired tackler's tale is the following one— and is supposedly absolutely true: One tackler, who used to take his homing pigeon to the local football match and release it before the match started. "A real tackler's trick", was the response of his friends, not realising he was sending his season ticket home to his brother, so he could get back in the ground free to watch the same game.

J.A.R

For Whom the Bell Tolls in the Fylde

THE Fylde area of land between the Wyre estuary north of Blackpool and the Ribble estuary—was once famous for the many windmills that dotted its flat landscape and several can still be seen today.

It was the custom that when a death occurred in the Fylde a whole district was invited to attend the funeral and help carry the coffin to the grave, often over great distances, using relays of coffin bearers. At a given hour the crowd assembled, not to mourn with the widow or orphan, but to drink beer, smoke and talk of their crops and dairies until the funeral was ready to begin.

From home and into and out of the church the coffin was carried on the shoulders of four relatives. The nearest relation, who acted as chief mourner, walked in front with the clegyman. When the service was over, sprigs of rosemary and box were thrown upon the coffin with a sprinkling of dust.

The whole company was then asked by the parish clerk to show their further respect for the dead by attending a dinner at the village inn. It was this event which sadly, so frequently developed into a drunken orgy that often made a Fylde funeral a matter of sad notoriety.

One pleasant aspect, however, of these old-time funerals was the distribution of doles of money to the poor who were sometimes fed as well. In the case of the more well-off families, cloaks and other useful garments would be given to the poor in memory of the deceased.

In even earlier times the more respected inhabitants of the area were buried by candlelight. It was regarded as a sacred duty to show a lighted candle in the window of every house as the coffin passed through the streets towards the church for interment. And he was considered poor indeed who did not pay this tribute of respect.

Edwin Bowman was born in 1920 in Hambleton, one of the Fylde's small villages in the area known as Over Wyre, and in his excellent book "When Every Day Was Summer" he confirms that in the old days as a last gesture of dignity and respect, coffins were carried shoulder high, sometimes for considerable distances with relays of bearers in attendance to take over at intervals.

Touching on the death of his mother, he says that members of her family for generations had been borne shoulder high to their graves and there was never any doubt she would wish to break, or would break the continuity.

Mr. Bowman also recalls working in the fields as a young man and hearing the 'passing bell' toll. "It was a familiar sound, sonorous and solemn reminding us all of our mortality . . . It reached out over the several square miles from the tower of Hambleton Church, just across the fields from where I was.

"Always we knew for whom the bell tolled, unless there had been an unexpected fatality. This time it was for Mr. Salisbury a farmer of formidable bearing and great conviction . . . As was the custom of all peasants who toiled out their long days in the fields, surrounded by nature and exposed to all her rigours, I paused, leant on my fork and gave a thought for his passing".

Earlier this century a well-known Fleetwood charwoman, Mrs. Ann Bullen, gave more than a thought for her passing. She made preparations for her own funeral by purchasing a grave in Fleetwood cemetery and having her name inscribed on the headstone with the date of death left blank.

Mrs. Bullen also placed on the headstone the name of one of her daughters—Janey—who had

Fleetwood charwoman, Ann Bullen (1842-1911), standing beside her own grave in 1908.

predeceased her. And that wasn't all. In a letter deposited with her solicitor, she gave instructions that there should be no flowers and no hearse.

Money had been left to cover the services of 12 bearers for her coffin, stipulating that there should be relays of four to carry it from her home to the cemetery.

Final instructions were that she wished to be buried wearing her best silk dress, gold earrings, stockings and boots.

Today all signs of tangible evidence that Ann Bullen, hardworking charwoman of Fleetwood, ever existed have disappeared forever from the windswept old Church of England section of Fleetwood Cemetery.

Now only the brief words "Ann Bullen (Grave No.6A)

buried 27th February, 1911, aged 69 years" permanently recorded in the Cemetery Records of Wyre Borough Council, testify that she lived and died.

In 1991, eighty years after Ann Bullen's death, in the Fylde village of Layton, near Blackpool pensioner Bert Thompson has also prepared for the inevitable.

Bert, a 68-year-old bachelor, bought himself a plot in Layton Cemetery after hearing that "the cemetery was filling up rapidly and I didn't want to be left out".

Bert's headstone, in grey polished granite, carries the inscription "In Loving Memory of Gilbert Charles (Bert) Thompson". followed by "Died" (blank space) and "Aged" (blank space).

The plot and headstone was bought with some money that Bert had put by for a rainy day and is positioned just feet away from the grave of a drinking pal.

E.C.

Photo copyright of The Evening Gazette, Blackpool.

Gilbert Charles (Bert) Thompson, of Layton, near Blackpool born 1923, pictured in January 1991, fully prepared for death.

The Pig Killer

WILLIAM Arrowsmith was a youth of 17 when he first took up pig killing and 65 years later was still following his trade as a travelling country pig butcher.

Born in 1834 not far from Bickerstaffe Church, near Ormskirk, he was known as "Owd Penketh" by the residents of Up Holland, Holland Moor, Digmoor, Crawford Village, Rainford and Skelmersdale, which he visited regularly.

In his prime he could kill about 12 pigs in a day, a fine achievement when one considers he had to travel to farms and cottages mainly on foot, between each kill. William once stated proudly: "I've walked from Digmoor (where he lived) to Frank Mercer's at Pimbo Lane and had two pigs killed before breakfast". He was also fond of saying that his work was to "find summat for t'bally an' somebody else can look after t'back".

Apart from food for the family, local boys and girls too, became excited at the prospect of a pig killing visit by "Owd Penketh". For if they were lucky, the end result would be an inflated pig's bladder to be used as a football.

Pork products were popular in the mill towns and vil-

Country pig butcher, William Arrowsmith, alias "Owd Penketh" of Digmoor, still carrying out his life's work at the age of 82. Of him it was said: "The number of porkers that have succumbed to his blandishments is legion."

lages of Lancashire and long before the Industrial Revolution the pig figured largely in the Lancashire diet. As well as the indispensible 'collops of fat bacon', and ham shanks, favourite dishes were black puddings and pigs trotters.

To make black puddings, when a pig was killed its blood was collected in a bucket and stirred—traditionally with the arm up to the elbow—until it coagulated and darkened. To it were added groats and pieces of fat about the size of dice, and herbs for flavouring. Black puddings were made from the skins of the intestines and at first resembled fat sausages. By the time the ends had been drawn and tied together the general appearance was spherical.

Trotters consisted of the edible parts of the pig's foot, boiled at the tripe works, with the cleaves torn away by a special hook. It resembled a mass of transparent jelly, slightly yellow in colour.

The year 1893 proved to be "Owd Penketh's" busiest time. A coal strike took place which was to last 16 weeks. Colliers in his catchment area, who were lucky enough to have something in the sty to kill, were then glad to be rid of their porkers.

In that 16-week period he killed no less than 500 pigs "to help 'em find summat t'eat", he modestly stated at the time.

Our photograph, taken from an old newspaper cutting shows "Owd Penketh" with his latest victim. The photograph was taken at the rear of the Bowling Green Inn, Digmoor, near Skelmersdale, where he had, as usual carried out the task of killing with surgical precision on behalf of the then landlord, Robert Kenyon.

Unlike any of the thousands of his past 'victims', William Arrowsmith died peacefully in his bed at the age of 83, on 13th February, 1917, at Pemberton, near Wigan.

J.P.

The Most Haunted County in England

by Sally Wallbank

LANCASHIRE is reputed to be the most haunted county in the whole of England. For hundreds of years ordinary Lancashire folk have witnessed boggarts, the English word for poltergeists. Lives have been turned upside down, as well as belongings, for boggarts are mischievous. Pots and pans as well as dishes are often seen to fly through the air—even the odd cat or two!

In the olden days the well-known cure to get rid of a boggart was to feed it regularly with a saucer of milk left on the doorstep. If you followed this rule and stuck to it the boggart would be at peace with you.

Well known to the people of Lancashire as Witch country is Pendle Hill. Ordinary folk at one time only took the path through Pendle Forest in the day time—and even then shadows of every size and shape blocked out the sun above. The witches of Pendle were spoken of with fear, and many people who entered the forest were never heard of again. Word soon spread throughout Lancashire and the witches' reputation rapidly grew stronger.

People still point out the little circular window in Crow Cottage in Worston, and the all-seeing eye on the Buddhist temple on the church tower of the new church in Pendle—at one time known as Goldshaw Booth "Witch Window Village".

Pendle's most feared witch was Demdike, but she was tried along with other reputed witches and put to death.

* * * *

A believer in the supernatural, who had always sought proof, wrote to me about his experience one night at the factory in Manchester where he worked as a boilerman.

He had not worked there long as he had spent years at sea in the navy where he had come across many harrowing and dangerous situations. His job at the factory (known locally as Rubberoid) involved shift work which he did not mind.

This particular night he began to feel a little on edge but couldn't as they say, put his finger on it. He was on the late shift and said goodnight to the worker he was relieving who seemed eager to be home.

Things at the factory seemed very disturbed but, once again, he could not think why this should be so. A few hours passed and he decided to have a drink from his flask and read a book. He had not been sat down long when he felt uneasy and looking up saw a man standing in front of his desk. His story goes on: "The man never spoke but just kept looking at me. I had never seen him before and for a moment my mind slipped and I thought it was time for me to be relieved. But the time for me to go home was 6.15 and it was only 5.15.

"By this time I felt and sensed fear. The man in front of the desk slowly turned to walk away and I decided he must have been an intruder. Lifting my chair, I threw it at the man. He was solid of appearance, but the chair went right through him.

"By this time I knew what I had seen was no human being. He, at this point, had just vanished. I sat by my desk numb and waited for my workmate. When he arrived he asked me what was the matter and said 'You look like you have seen THE ghost'. I remember making a mental note of what he had just said—THE ghost and not A ghost.

"He asked me to describe what I had seen in every detail—the curly ginger hair and the shirt collar sewn at the back to stop the edges fraying. 'You have seen the ghost' said my workmate. 'From time to time he comes back to the factory to relieve his mate no matter who it is'.

"I asked who 'he' or 'it' was and found out he used to work at the factory and one day killed himself, but still relieves workers at 5.15—the time shifts used to be changed".

* * * *

This true ghostly tale was told me by an ex-Serviceman.

"Around midnight I was returning home to Liverpool on the last ferry boat after seeing my fiance home safely.

I had to walk the rest of the way as it was late (the last bus having already long since gone) and decided to choose the route home with the best street lighting as it was now quite dark.

I made my way via Borough Road to Liscard Road and upon reaching St. John's Church opposite the junction with Church Street, saw that the pavement ahead, which runs alongside Central Park, was very dark and shaded with overhanging trees. I decided to cross the road to the other pavement beyond the Church Street junction.

The weather conditions were perfectly still and no other person was about. As I reached the pavement I became aware of a small, solid, dark figure coming through the railings which surround the church and ancient graveyard.

It was a man dressed as a Puritan with a tall hat, and black cloak. His hands, clasped in front, were shielding a candle, the light of which illuminated the whole of his dark face revealing a large nose, and enough for me to realise that he was looking across the road at me. I quickened my steps but he kept level.

It occurred to me to cross over the road for a further inspection, but I decided against this, and quickened my steps once more. At this point he let out a high pitched half-laugh scream, rising in crescendo and I took off like an Olympic runner.

I thought I had seen every horror there was to see during my war but on looking back it appeared I had not. I've never seen anything like it before or since and I never want to see such a thing like it again.

Living here in Liverpool all my life I have noticed over the years that on that junction there are always a lot of accidents—on the very spot I witnessed this 'being'.

I often wonder if I had crossed the road all those years ago would I have become another accident statistic?

* * * *

Finally with so many reported ghostly experiences and sightings around the county, I decided to do some research into all aspects of the paranormal, but where to begin?

I decided if I was going to do some serious research then Britain's most haunted house was the place to be so I contacted the owners of Chingle Hall, John and Sandra Bruce. My first adventure had begun.

Chingle, despite being the most haunted house in Britain, has a fascinating history attached to it and will explain how some of the ghosts came to be at the hall.

Built in the year 1260 by a young knight, Adam de Singleton, it was owned by the de Singletons and the Wall family (both sides of the families related) throughout its sometimes turbulant history.

During the 15th century Chingle was to witness a big change in religion. Queen Elizabeth I wanted only her own faith to be the faith of England and, deciding to be guided by the Church of England, gave monks and priests a chance to live if they gave up their Catholic faith. Some did, but not the monks and priests of Chingle Hall.

Chingle Hall sits sturdy, white walled and cruciform behind its moat, Built 1260 by Adam De Singleton, with chapel and three priest hides. Written in Domm Bede Camm's book "Forgotten Shrines" and other Catholic records as the birthplace of St. John Wall (1620)

They gave their own lives by either protecting the Hall's owners or by refusing to give up their faith. During these turbulant times it was against the Queen's wishes for anyone to be found practising any other faith than her own and any who were found to be practising it, would be put to death on the spot.

Chingle's ghosts range from monks, priests, women, cavaliers, children, the children often died through illnesses but still have been seen to play at the hall. Probably the most famous ghost is St. John Wall, born at Chingle in 1620 to become one of England's last martyrs. He became a Franciscan priest but when his faith caught up with him by being seen and recognized by a soldier he was captured and hung in 1679. His head is still said to be somewhere in Chingle.

Chingle's family ties broke continuity in 1794 when the Faringtons became the new owners. They lived there for a good few hundred years and then the Hall seemed to be without owners until a local couple, a Mr. and Mr. Howarth, decided to rent it before buying it in 1959.

Years later Mr. Howarth died and Mrs. Howarth's sister came to live at the hall with her, but the two now old ladies were not disturbed by all the ghostly goings-on. After their deaths the hall again lay empty until John Bruce and his wife Sandra fell in love with Chingle and bought it in the 1980s. It does have that effect on you even though it is haunted; haunted not only on the stroke of midnight but during the day too.

If you would like more information on Chingle for a guided tour or an overnight stay give me a ring (0704 892639) or contact Chingle (0772 861 082).

● *Sally Wallbank lives at Burscough, near Ormskirk. She is psychic and bioelectrically sensitive, and has extensively researched the paranormal. She is regularly in demand by scientific institutions nationwide to further studies into the paranormal. In addition she is currently engaged in completing a manuscript on Chingle Hall—Britain's Most Haunted House, to be published in due course.*

The Melody Born of Pendle

by Albert Winstanley

Francis Duckworth (1862-1941).

THERE was a day in 1917, when a company of Lancashire Fusiliers were assembled on Mount Calvary. It was the Sunday following the capture of Jerusalem by the brilliant General Allenby. It was also the most moving of occasions, especially on this most hallowed spot the world has known, which is so deeply enshrined in our christian heritage.

It was appropriate that a simple but fitting Hymn of Praise should have been chosen and in swelling harmony and unison, the lusty voices of those Fusiliers joined in the singing of:-

"Jesus shall reign where'er the sun,
Doth his successive journeys run,
His Kingdom stretch from shore to shore,
Till moons shall wax, and wane no more".

As beautiful as the words sang that morning by Lancashire voices, so was the melody—a melody that echoed across from Calvary, to a little secluded village of Rimington in the Pendle area of Lancashire, after which it was named.

Every Lancastrian knows of Pendle Hill, with its bold and thrilling contours, which look so benignly down at the trim little villages in its shadow. Each and every village hoards and retains a story of yesterday—but, perhaps that of Rimington's is the lasting jewel of them all.

It all began on Christmas Day in 1862, when in the village, Francis Duckworth was born. He was only five years old, when the family moved to nearby Stopper Lane, where next door to the Wesleyan Chapel, his parents kept the village shop.

Those were the days when Sunday worship was an important part of life, and the singing of hymns was with a greater fervency than today. They were sung with gusto by the children of every village school, and by farming men at their labours in the fields. Who cannot fail to be enchanted by memory pictures of cottage scenes when the day's work was done; when in the mellow glow from candles and oil lamps, there would be family readings from the scriptures and the singing of favourite hymns.

The uncle of young Francis (his "Uncle Joe") was a devout 'Wesleyan' Methodist, and often on his visits to the Stopper Lane shop, he would discuss with other customers in the shop, the merits of the previous Sunday service in the chapel, and the hymns that had been sung. He loved the ancient hymn writers, especially the noted Isaac Watts, and one day in the shop during a discussion, he was "carried away" with his fervour.

He raised his hands, and in a deep eloquent voice proclaimed:

"Jesus shall reign where'er the sun!"

"Where'er the Sun" he repeated. "Do you know that that

means everybody everywhere's going to accept Him! Ah!— Watts had the conception, he said more in one line than a lot of them say in a whole hymn".

Unknowingly, the words had made a deep impression on the young Francis Duckworth, and he would never forget the scene that had taken place in the shop.

Though he led the life of a typical village boy, indulging in all the usual escapades sports and pastimes, and getting into 'mischief', he began to appreciate and love

The Rimington village shop and adjacent Methodist chapel (now a private house), where Francis Duckworth lived and worshipped.

music. His favourite instrument was the organ, and he eventually became an accomplished player.

Times were hard, however, and his mother died when he was only 12-years-old, and he had to leave school to take up employment. He worked for a cousin in a tobacco shop, and for six years for a brother as a printer, but in 1889 he opened a grocer's shop in Colne.

The business was a success and he was respected in the several towns and villages of the area. He became dedicated to the organ, and became the organist at Albert Road Wesleyan Church, an honorary position in which he served for 50 years. In this capacity he was composing music particularly for hymns, and in 1904 his hymn tune *Rimington* was published.

He had never forgotten the scene in the little shop at Stopper Lane, and his Uncle John enthusing about Watt's hymn. He was, therefore, to dedicate it to the village of his birth. It was sung for the first time in public in the same year at the Colne Whitsunside processions, and from there, the lilting melody was to spread throughout the world.

It was sung by a mass open-air congregation of 40,000 at Halifax, by 20,000 at Nelson, and at Pendleton by 22 massed choirs. Gramophone recordings followed, and it was to become a popular 'test piece' in the repertoire of Brass Bands everywhere.

More hymns tunes were to come from his gifted pen, but Rimington, was, undoubtedly his crowning glory. Not only does the melody capture to perfection the christian message of the words, it enshrines the beauty of the Pendle landscape where it was born.

Alas, the Wesleyan Chapel of Stopper Lane is now but a memory. It was converted to a private house some years ago, but a 'memory' plaque was placed in position on a wall to record the event.

I shall always treasure the memory of a day, when the chapel was open, and I opened the door to peep inside. Prominent was the organ on which Francis had so often played; now mute and silent.

There was no-one around, and almost on tip-toe I walked to the organ, and somehow I just had to sit down and play his *Rimington,* for I too had known the melody from my own boyhood days, and had played it often at the Sunday School classes I had attended on those far-away days. It was a most satisfying few moments.

Just 50 years ago, Francis Duckworth died at his home at Colne, on 16th August, 1941, in his 80th year. Inscribed on his gravestone in the churchyard of nearby St. Mary The Virgin, Gisburn, are a few bars of the words and music of *Rimington* in loving testimony to the melody born of Pendle that he bequeathed to the world.

● *A poem titled 'Rimington' has been penned by Christine Thistlethwaite of Rimington village, as a tribute to Francis Duckworth. Page 62.*

"Wm. Turton, Lancashire Clogs"

by Ellen Callon

"WM. TURTON, Lancashire Clogs" reads the handwritten sign on number 129 High Street in Old Skelmersdale.

The neat semi-detached house has been the home of Bill Turton for all his 60 years—37 of them as a clogmaker and now the only maker of clog soles in Lancashire.

With his wife Yvonne he runs the business from his workshops at the bottom of a well-kept garden and once inside the visitor is transported into a world of the craftsman of old.

Apparatus of all shapes and sizes takes up most of the space among the benches littered with clogging paraphernalia and sewing machines.

There's a 'skeiver' which trims the leather so it can be stitched; a splitting machine (thins the leather if it is too thick), zig-zagger (joins the back seams), toe tin press (presses the tin out to be nailed on the front of the clog) and another appliance that cuts out the uppers was purchased from a farmer in Ormskirk and is reputed to be more than 100 years old.

Standing in a corner is a drum-like piece of equipment

Bill Turton, Clog Maker, in his workshop at the rear of his home, and the only maker of clog soles in Lancashire

that Bill made himself and is called a waxer. Into this goes the cow hide after it has been dyed and it is heated so that the leather becomes completely impregnated in the wax. To this is added Bill's special secret ingredient which gives the leather its extra suppleness. On coming across a library book on the subject he produced his own waxer after much trial and error.

He went on: "But it's all been worth it. I've never wanted to do anything else but make clogs and it's been a good life".

Sentiments echoed by his wife. Both derive as much pride and enjoyment from their work today as when they started and have a perfect working relationship which complements their happy marriage. They discuss everything and are continually looking at ways of improving and updating their product. Yvonne considers their clogs are now as neat and light as can possibly be achieved.

Bill's craftsmanship was recognised in the 1991 Thwaites Achievement Awards, part of the Blackburn brewer's Perfectly Crafted Heritage Campaign which looks for people whose skills 'made the north great'. The awards were judged on the contribution made by individuals to society over a number of years and Bill came third, following winner Ron Carter, a blacksmith from Burnley and runner-up Edward Crowhurst, a wheelwright from Churchtown near Southport. He received £200 and a specially-struck ceramic Thwaites Achievement Plaque at a buffet dinner to honour the craftsmen.

The techniques of clogmaking were passed on to Bill by Fred Jones of Wigan. Bill's father Tom (he died in 1962) was a stitcher at the Skelmersdale Shoe Factory, but it was clogs that fascinated young Bill and when he left school at 14, he became apprenticed to the Co-op in Skelmersdale in the days when most Co-ops had a clogging service, serving seven years under Fred.

On his 21st birthday he received 'calling up' papers for National Service and carried on his trade, as well as shoe repairing, in the Army. When he came out two years later he returned to the Co-op for a period of only three months he had already decided to work on his own.

Yvonne had come into his life by then. He met her at a dance at Wigan's Empress Hall four days after he was demobbed. She was then employed in the cutting room of a Wigan factory that made sportswear, and although she nurtured an ambition to become a nurse joined Bill in his venture.

He had made the right decision. There was plenty of work and today they have enough orders to keep them busy round the clock. Mainly wholesalers, they supply the other 24 clogmakers in the country with uppers and now soles. In fact the majority buy everything from them.

In charge of making the soles is daughter Sandra, expertly taught by dad. A former hairdresser, she sold her business when daughters Kirsty, now seven, and six-year-old Claire were born, but she was always a frequent caller at the workshops. She says: "I was bored at home and used to come for afternoons helping where I could and it developed from there.

Nine different clog styles are made in the workshops, among them the Derby (named after Lord Derby who had them made for his workers) and the Dandy, a decorated clog used by morris dancing troupes. The decorative work is done with a crimping tool.

Then there is the lace—a ladies and gents clog for walking or gardening etc; the long tongued (a bit fancier); the Deshu which has a strap instead of a buckle and the tongue is attached; the button clog and the bar. Popular among the souvenir hunters is the clasp clog, the oldest design of all and worn by millworkers and miners in an era when you could tell the time of day by the clatter of clogs on the setts.

Bill once made special clog soles out of ash for a Wigan dancing troupe travelling to Germany but beech is now the main wood used. This has gradually replaced alder, which was the best wood for clogs because of its resistance to moisture and the fact that it does not split easily.

Found in marshes and along the middle rivers, alder became less available as drainage of land was carried out and many rivers were either controlled or reduced. But beech has been an admirable substitute as it is moderately hard, even-grained and lends itself to carving.

Trees only become available through natural wastage so Bill has three or four outlets that supply him with beech which is cut when wet. After he has taken delivery it is stacked outside and left to dry naturally.

Black used to be the predominate colour for clogs but

now there's a more colourful demand—brown, red, green and blue. Sandra has a green pair complete with safety cap (all clogs conform to British safety standards) and her daughters wear red ones. "I always know where they are when they have their clogs on", laughed Sandra, who has given their range of children's clogs the artistic touch by handpainting flowers, butterflies and even turtles on them.

Every year brings a full diary of outings to various town and county shows up and down the country as Bill joins other craftsmen demonstrating their age-old skills. Some of them such as the Royal Lancashire show, Southport Flower Show and the Westmorland Show are in conjunction with the Heritage Campaign.

It's a wonderful opportunity for visitors to see Bill at work and no matter where he goes there will always be someone to say: "I never knew there were people still making clogs".

Talk of retirement and Bill shakes his head. "We'll never retire. This is a way of life more than a job of work and I'll never give it up. I just love making clogs. It's a lovely thing is a clog. A beautiful shape that's been produced from a side of leather and a piece of wood. And when you've finished it and look at it you say 'I've made that and it's good; it's right. There's no other feeling like it".

Bill is keen to preserve and pass on his skills and has thoughts of starting a school for clogmakers. He said: "The only snag is the cost. About £5,000 would be needed for equipment. But clogmaking must not die out. It's got to keep going".

The master craftsman has no worries about the future of "Wm. Turton, Lancashire Clogs" for his daughter plans to keep the business alive. "I shall never let it go", she said. "It's my heritage".

'Pressed' to Death

MANY and varied have been the tortures and punishments devised for wrongdoing. So much so, that up to the 18th century, it seemed that the variety of tortures and punishments almost matched the number of types of crimes.

One particularly horrific and barbaric torture carried out at Lancaster Castle and elsewhere, was known by the insignificant word of "Pressing"—*peine forte et dure.*

"Pressing" was carried out by stripping bare the prisoner, apart from his or her loins, then lying on their backs, outstretched arms and legs were bound with tightly drawn cords attached to iron staples driven into the ground. A board was then placed on the prisoner's chest and weights prescribed by law, were consecutively placed on the board until the number of weights caused the victim to die slowly of suffocation. Sometimes prisoners begged for mercy to plead guilty to the charge, in which case they were hanged.

The decision to carry out "pressing" was specifically reserved for prisoners who refused to "stand to the law", which meant prisoners who refused to plead to a particular

A 19th century engraving of one Wm. Spiggot under pressure for not pleading to his indictment

crime or prisoners who remained mute.

The reason for so many prisoners refusing to readily plead in answer to a charge, was because an ancient law decreed that if prisoners did not plead to a charge of crime, then their property could not be confiscated by the Crown.

In the reign of Henry IV (1367-1413), such persons were condemned to penance and perpetual imprisonment; in fact the penance meant confinement in a narrow cell and absolute starvation. Eventually a more awful form of torture was devised with the object of compelling the silent to speak.

If a prisoner continued not to plead, the sentence of *"Peine forte et dure* was passed upon the prisoner with the following words:

> "That you be taken back to the prison whence you came to a low dungeon, into which no light can enter; that you be laid on your back on the bare floor with a cloth round your loins, but elsewhere naked; that there be set upon your body a weight of iron as great as you can bear—and greater; that you have no sustenance, save on the first day three morsels of the coarsest bread, on the second day three draughts of stagnant water from the pool nearest to the prison door, on the third day again three morsels of bread as before, and such bread and such water alternately from day to day till you die".

J.P.

Lancashire Books through the eyes of Bob Dobson

I HAVE been involved in the world of Lancashire books for over twenty years and unless I'm very much mistaken, things have not been worse than during the year of 1991. The 'recession' is at the heart of it. Shops are selling fewer books, paying their bills slower and having little in the way of confidence to pass on to publishers of Lancashire-interest books. In turn, this lack of confidence "Will I get my money back?" is passed on from publisher to author. I am aware of several authors who have had their manuscripts returned by cautious publishers. Whilst pre-Christmas sales will help the situation, it will not restore this lost confidence.

Only in Manchester, the most book-conscious Lancashire town, is the book scene vibrant. Several shops have closed in the last year, but been replaced by others. The big boys of bookselling, Waterstone's and Dillon's have taken on increased space to sell their wares, though I'm sad to say their stock has little to interest those seeking Lancashire material.

However, all is not doom and gloom. There are some good things planned for the Lancashire book buyer in the field of Lancashire books, and there have been some highlights appearing on bookshelves in the last year or so. I'll tell you of some of these first:-

Carnegie Publishing are probably the most active publisher of Lancashire history books. They have recently formed an association with the Lancashire Library Service, which means their list of titles is available in every Lancashire County Library. Of their recent titles, I have especially enjoyed Mike Clarke's **The Leeds & Liverpool Canal**. It will become the standard work on the subject. Of equal status are Peter Aughton's **Southport Story** and David Hunt's **History of Preston** due out. It will be an important contribution to Preston's proud past. Of their other titles I'm also impressed with Dean Hayes' **Lancashire Cricketing Greats** and with John Hanavy's **Historic Wigan**.

***

T.H.C.L. Books are a small company with a big reputation. Their main field of interest is in military matters, but they have also enriched the local books scene. Often their publications have been on Lancashire military subjects such as **The Seven V.C's of Stonyhurst College** but their important contribution has been in the local history field. I commend Abram's **History of Blackburn**, a reprint of the 1887 edition and I look forward to the reprint of Shaw's **Darwen & Its People**. They have re-published George Miller's **Byegone Blackburn** and plan to publish his **Evolution of a Cotton town**.

***

Picks are used by miners. Picks Publishing is the trading name of Ian Winstanley, who writes and publishes mining titles with a strong Lancashire flavour. He has recently written **With Hearts So Light,** the story of the Queen Pit Explosions at Haydock in 1868/9. He intends to follow his work with Geoff Simm - **Mining Memories, An Illustrated Record of Mining in St. Helens 1540-1990,** a splendid contribution to local history. Ian plans more books on mining both nationally and locally. He collects material on all mining disasters.

***

Manchester publisher Neil Richardson has been producing valuable local history gems for many years. He is both printer and publisher, a rare combination. In recent times, many of his titles have leaned towards military matters, though he still keeps bringing out books on pubs, canals, and remains very strong on biographies of Lancashire people. Neil and his wife Sue are also authors. Their **Fallen In the Fight** gives biographies of over 700 Farnworth and Kearsley men who died in World War I and expands to tell of the battles. It is given some heart touching quality by the addition of some letters from the soldiers at the front. Neil's publications are mostly of interest to those in Greater Manchester. He plans books on Belle Vue and on Samuel Bamford.

***

Printwise Publications have until recently been responsible for bringing other publishers' books to the shops very cheaply—known in the trade as remainders dealers. However, they embarked on a new line of publishing their own titles in the last year and have produced **Ports of the North West, Southport in Focus, Bright and Breezy Blackpool** all by Catherine Rothwell amongst their titles. If you are seeing books selling in the shops at much less than their published prices, it is through the efforts of Printwise's Sales Director, Cliff Hayes.

* * *

Owl Books of Wigan have an impressive, if short, list of titles under their belt. Although their best sellers have been **Chilling True Tales of Old Preston** by Keith Johnson and **Ghosts, Mysteries and Legends of Old Warrington (Books 1 and 2)** by Wally Barnes. My pick of their publications is Edwin Bowman's **When Every Day Was Summer** a social history of the Over Wyre village of Hambleton 1920-39. It captivated me. I found a lot of pleasure too in **Golden Days Awheel** by Albert Winstanley, a veteran cyclist, though not all of the book concerns Lancashire lanes.

Also from the Wigan stable under the Coveropen imprint comes **Albert's Easy Teach Yourself Lancashire Dialect**, compiled by Ernie Ford of Westhoughton. Not to be taken seriously, the stories and cartoons are in the Lancashire lingo, together with 150 word Lanky/Standard English dictionery which could rival Andy Capp. The booklet is based on an archetypal pipe-smoking Lancashire character called 'Albert', who comes complete with flat cap, union shirt and silk muffler.

* * *

Landy Publishing is my imprint. Over the past year I have edited and published several books in a series bearing the name of various Lancashire towns **Blackburn, Bury, Lancaster, Wigan, Chorley, Bolton, Blackpool and Fleetwood—A Century Ago.** They are based on a trades directory of the towns first published in 1889, and have introductory essays by local historians. I plan to continue this series with books on Preston, Southport and Manchester. Following on the publication a year ago of a dialect poetry anthology, **From Lancashire Lips,** I plan another to be called **In Lancashire Language.** More dialect poetry is to be found in Margaret Helliwell's **Valley Verses**

There are other companies publishing Lancashire books. Most books do get reviewed in the quarterly magazine of the Lancashire Author's Association and often in *Lancashire Life,* the *Lancashire Magazine* and *Red Rose Magazine.*

In the world of secondhand books there is much activity. Shops have recently opened up in such unlikely places as Oswaldtwistle, Haslingden, Bacup and Wigan, though sadly one closed in Lancaster and Chorley. Lancashire is well served with Secondhand Book Fairs (run by myself and the Provincial Book Fairs Association).

Addresses of the publishers and others mentioned above:

Carnegie Publishing, 18 Maynard Street, Preston PR2 2AL.

T.H.C.L. Books, 185 Lammack Road, Blackburn BB1 8LH.

Picks Publishing, 83 Greenfields Crescent, Ashton-in-Makerfield, Wigan WN4 8QY.

Neil Richardson, 88 Ringley Road, Stoneclough, Radcliffe M26 9ET.

Printwise Publications Ltd., 41 Willan Estate, Vere Street, Salford M5 2GR.

Landy Publishing, 3 Staining Rise, Staining, Blackpool FY3 0BU.

Owl Books, P.O. Box 60, Wigan WN1 2QB.

Lancashire Authors Association (Eric Holt, Secretary), 5 Quaker Fields, Westhoughton, Bolton BL5 2BJ.

Lancashire Life Magazine, Oyston Mill, Strand Road, Preston.

Lancashire Magazine, Barclays Bank Chambers, Sowerby Bridge, HX6 2DX.

Red Rose Magazine, 48 Hall Carr Road, Rossendale.

Provincial Book Fairs Association (P.B.F.A.), The Old Coach House, 16 Melbourn Street, Royston SG8 7BX.